This Planner Belongs To:

....

....

Plannner Introduction

Welcome to the Peak Productivity Planner!

My name is Jari Roomer and I'm the founder of Personal Growth Lab. At Personal Growth Lab, you can find anything you need to upgrade your productivity, achieve your goals, and work with laser-focus.

One of my core beliefs is that action takers win in life. Everyone has dreams and goals, but most people fail to make them a reality simply because they don't take consistent, focused action towards those goals. This is where the Peak Productivity Planner comes in!

My primary goal with this planner is to help you get stuff done - in a focused and time-efficient way - so you can make massive progress towards your goals. Whether you're a high-level CEO, entrepreneur, writer, student, or anything in between, this planner will help you get unstoppable momentum, crush your daily to-dos, and reach maximum productivity.

Through years of development, the Peak Productivity Planner is specifically designed to help you get more done using smart productivity techniques. By using this planner on a daily basis, you'll structure your days and weeks, stay focused on your goals & priorities, and be motivated to take consistent action. All in all, it's your companion for success.

Excited already? Let's dive into how to best use this planner!

"Productivity is never an accident. It is always the result of a commitment to excellence, intelligent planning, and focused effort."
- Paul J. Meyer

Planner Explanation

Before you start your productivity journey, it's important to know exactly how to use this planner for maximum results.

So, what can you expect?

For a period of 10 weeks (70 days), you'll have the opportunity to 10X your productivity. This requires the commitment and consistency to use this planner every single day. Even on your free days, use this planner to ensure it becomes an unbreakable daily habit.

The Peak Productivity Planner consists of four different components:
1. Setting Your 10-Week Goal(s)
2. Weekly Productivity Pages
3. Daily Productivity Pages
4. Example Pages

Setting Your 10-Week Goal(s)

To help you get the most out of the next 10 weeks, I recommend you set at least one goal that you want to achieve during this period. Having a few clear goals to work towards during this 10-week period will help you work with better focus and stronger motivation. Therefore, in the upcoming section, we've got a few questions prepared to help you set these goals.

Weekly Productivity Pages

Planning your weeks is essential for maximum productivity. Therefore, we've included weekly productivity pages after each week. In this component, you can reflect on your performance of the past week and prepare for a productive week ahead.

For example, you'll be asked to set your top 3 goals for the next week, schedule your days, and track your most important habits. These exercises will make your weeks exponentially more productive and successful.

Daily Productivity Pages

The daily productivity pages will have the biggest impact on your productivity. These pages are designed to help you reach peak productivity on a daily basis. For example, you'll be asked to review your long-term goals, create your ABCDE list, and schedule your day in detail. Furthermore, at the end of the day, you'll be asked to reflect on your performance so you can improve every single day.

You'll notice that this planner doesn't include a normal to-do list component. If you've been following Personal Growth Lab for a while, this doesn't come as a surprise. The thing is, although a to-do list is a very popular productivity tool, it's far from complete. The problem with a to-do list is that it doesn't indicate which to-do items are highly important and which ones are much less important. This often leads to a false sense of productivity. Therefore, I'd prefer to use something called the ABCDE Method.

If you're not familiar with the ABCDE Method, let me explain:

I like to call the ABCDE List a 'to-do list on steroids' as it looks like a normal to-do list, but it's actually a much stronger productivity tool. Instead of a normal to-do list, an ABCDE List actually indicates which tasks are your priorities and which tasks aren't. This ensures you focus more on the things that truly matter, which is key in maximizing your productivity.

Applying the ABCDE method requires two simple steps:
1. Just like with a to-do list, start by writing down all the items that you want to get done today.
2. Assign either an A, B, C, D, or E to each of the items on your list.

Step 1 is the easy part, but **step 2** is a bit harder. Let's take a look at what all these different letters mean.

A-Tasks: These tasks are mission-critical. They have the most impact and contribute the most to the achievement of your goals, so you should make it a priority to accomplish these tasks no matter what. Keep your A-Tasks at a maximum of three per day to keep optimal focus.

B-Tasks: These tasks are important, but not as important as your A-Tasks. You'd want to finish these tasks, but not at the cost of your A-Tasks.

C-Tasks: These tasks aren't essential at all. It might be nice to get them done today, but they should never get in the way of your A-Tasks or B-Tasks.

D-Tasks: These tasks can be delegated to someone who can do it faster, cheaper, or better. Your time should be spend on more valuable tasks.

E-Tasks: These tasks can be eliminated from your day. Maybe they can be accomplished tomorrow.

You can further prioritize these tasks by using numbers (1, 2 and 3) to indicate which task is the most important within a category. For example, an A1 task is more important than an A2 or A3 task.

By using the ABCDE Method, you rank your daily tasks based on their priority. This is essential for maximum productivity as it helps you focus on the tasks that truly have an impact. At the same time, it makes sure you don't get distracted by the tasks that matter less.

All in all, creating an ABCDE List will help you be a lot more productive compared to using a normal to-do list! You'll find out soon enough when you start using the planner.

Example Pages

For the sake of clarity, this planner includes a few 'example pages'. These pages show you clear examples of how to use this planner on a daily and weekly basis, which removes any potential ambiguity.

Now that we've got the basics of the Peak Productivity Planner covered, it's time to get started! Once again, I highly recommend using this planner every single day. This way, it becomes an unbreakable daily habit, which leads to the best results.

With that being said, good luck, enjoy the experience, and let's get some stuff done!

Jari Roomer

Founder Personal Growth Lab

"Success can only be achieved through consistent daily action. It's what we do day-to-day, even when no one is looking, that determines our reality."
- Jari Roomer

Example Pages

Creating Your 10-Week Goal

To get the most out of the upcoming ten weeks, consider setting 1-3 goals that you want to achieve before the end of week 10. By setting one or more specific goals, you improve your focus and motivation for the upcoming period - both will benefit your productivity and performance.

 Goal-Setting Tip: Always make sure your goals are highly specific and measurable. For example, '*I want to write a lot for my book*' isn't a specific or measurable goal. A much better goal would be '*I will write 25,000 words for my book*'. The more specific the goal, the better you can measure your progress. The better you can measure your progress, the more likely you are to achieve your goal.

What 1-3 goals, if achieved, would lead me to consider this 10-week period to be a big success?

1. *Reached the B2-level Spanish proficiency*

2. *Doubled my productivity (Do 8 hours of work in 4 hours compared to today)*

3. *Reached 500 email subscribers for my new blog*

For each of the goals above, write down at least 3 reasons why achieving this goal is important to you (eg. how will achieving this goal improve your life?)

Goal 1	Goal 2	Goal 3
I want to live in Spain for a year.	*Create more free time to spend with close friends*	*Potential new passive income stream*
My family has Spanish roots	*Improve my focus to create more quality work*	*Share valuable knowledge with others*
I want to be able to watch Spanish movies	*Improve my chances to get a raise/promotion*	*Writing is a great way to learn new things*

Weekly Reflection *- Example*

Did I achieve my top 3 goals of the week? If not, why not?

This week, I did not manage to keep myself from checking social media during working hours. Although my phone was out of sight, I could not resist the temptation to check for any updates.

What lessons did I learn this week that I can use to make next week better?

Meditating in the morning has helped me become more mindful of when I have the urge to procrastinate. This makes me more productive.

What I've also noticed is that regular physical exercise has a positive impact on my mental clarity. And it feels good!

What am I proud of this week?

Remove all social media apps from my phone, or use an app-blocker. This will help me stay away from distractions during working hours.

I also want to take more time reading my Spanish book to accelerate my learning. 20 pages instead of 10 pages a day next week.

Notes:

Tracking my habits really helps me consistently do them while enjoying them more as well. It feels good to tick the boxes on my tracker!

Weekly Preparation *- Example*

My top 3 goals of this week are:

1. *Finished the first 2 modules of the digital marketing online course*

2. *Not checked social media during work once!*

3. *Read the first chapter of my new Spanish book*

Weekly Schedule

Monday	Tuesday	Wednesday
Watch module 1 of the digital marketing course	Learn 25 new Spanish words Do groceries for rest of the week	Write a blog post about personal finance.

Thursday	Friday	Weekend
Play tennis with a friend Learn 25 new Spanish Words	Watch module 2 of the digital marketing course	Movie night with friends Visit grandparents Schedule next week

Habit Tracker

	Mo	Tu	We	Th	Fr	Sa	Su
Green Juice Breakfast	X	X		X		X	
Meditate		X	X	X		X	X
Morning Journal	X	X	X	X	X	X	X
Go for a Run	X			X	X		X
Read 10 pages	X	X	X			X	X

Daily Preparation — *Example*

Goal Review:

I will live in Spain one day, connect with the locals, and experience their culture on a deeper level.

> *"For changes to be of any true value, they've got to be lasting and consistent."*
> — Tony Robbins

My ABCDE List

A-Tasks:

1. *Discuss promotion with boss*
2. *Send welcome email to new client*
3. *Pay overdue incoice*

B-Tasks:

1. *Set new deadline work-project*
2. *Reschedule today's meeting*
3. *Ask co-worker about contract*

C-Tasks:

1. *Check all email*
2. *Recharge car parking card*
3. *Prepare presentation next week*

D-Tasks:

1. *Replace light bulb desk lamp*
2. *Try out new company software*
3. *Solve keyboard error*

E-Tasks:

1. *Clean desktop homepage*
2. *Create new music playlist*
3. *Buy new pens and paper*

My Daily Schedule

05:00	
05:30	
06:00	
06:30	*Take a shower*
07:00	*Meditate and Write in Journ*
07:30	*Learn 25 Spanish words*
08:00	*Breakfast & Leave for Work*
08:30	
09:00	
09:30	
10:00	
10:30	
11:00	*Work through all my work-er*
11:30	
12:00	*Have lunch with co-workers*
12:30	
13:00	

Notes:

Reviewing my long term goals really helps me stay inspired and motivated the rest of the day!

13:30	
14:00	
14:30	
15:00	*Work meeting with colleague*
15:30	
16:00	
16:30	
17:00	*Last look at work-email*
17:30	
18:00	
18:30	*Dinner with roommates*
19:00	
19:30	
20:00	*Watch Module 1 DM course*
20:30	*Finish writing blog post*
21:00	*Daily Reflection*
21:30	

Daily Reflection

If I had to rate my day (1-10): __7.5__

Did I achieve my top priorities today? If not, why not?

I didn't manage to learn 25 new Spanish words because of a lack of time in the morning. I might have to plan that for the evening or get up earlier from now on.

What lessons did I learn today that I can use to make tomorrow a better day?

Checking my email only twice during the day really helps me stay focused on my more important tasks.

Go to bed earlier. A lack of sleep is really harming my focus during the the rest of the day.

What am I proud of today?

I finished writing my blog post!

End Example Pages

Notes:

....

....

....

....

....

....

| 13:30 |
| 14:00 |
| 14:30 |
| 15:00 |
| 15:30 |
| 16:00 |
| 16:30 |
| 17:00 |
| 17:30 |
| 18:00 |
| 18:30 |
| 19:00 |
| 19:30 |
| 20:00 |
| 20:30 |
| 21:00 |
| 21:30 |

Daily Reflection

If I had to rate my day (1–10): _____

Did I achieve my top priorities today? If not, why not?

....

....

....

....

....

What lessons did I learn today that I can use to make tomorrow a better day?

....

....

....

....

....

What am I proud of today?

....

....

....

....

Daily Preparation

Today's Date: ___ / ___ / ___

Goal Review:

....

....

....

My ABCDE List

A-Tasks:

1. ....

2. ....

3. ....

B-Tasks:

1. ....

2. ....

3. ....

C-Tasks:

1. ....

2. ....

3. ....

D-Tasks:

1. ....

2. ....

3. ....

E-Tasks:

1. ....

2. ....

3. ....

My Daily Schedule

Time	
05:00	
05:30	
06:00	
06:30	
07:00	
07:30	
08:00	
08:30	
09:00	
09:30	
10:00	
10:30	
11:00	
11:30	
12:00	
12:30	
13:00	

Notes:

....

....

....

....

....

....

13:30
14:00
14:30
15:00
15:30
16:00
16:30
17:00
17:30
18:00
18:30
19:00
19:30
20:00
20:30
21:00
21:30

Daily Reflection

If I had to rate my day (1-10): _____

Did I achieve my top priorities today? If not, why not?

....

....

....

....

....

....

What lessons did I learn today that I can use to make tomorrow a better day?

....

....

....

....

....

What am I proud of today?

....

....

....

....

Daily Preparation

Today's Date: ___ /___ /___

Goal Review:

....

....

....

My ABCDE List

A-Tasks:

1. ....

2. ....

3. ....

B-Tasks:

1. ....

2. ....

3. ....

C-Tasks:

1. ....

2. ....

3. ....

D-Tasks:

1. ....

2. ....

3. ....

E-Tasks:

1. ....

2. ....

3. ....

My Daily Schedule

Time
05:00
05:30
06:00
06:30
07:00
07:30
08:00
08:30
09:00
09:30
10:00
10:30
11:00
11:30
12:00
12:30
13:00

Notes:

....

....

....

....

....

....

13:30	
14:00	
14:30	
15:00	
15:30	
16:00	
16:30	
17:00	
17:30	
18:00	
18:30	
19:00	
19:30	
20:00	
20:30	
21:00	
21:30	

Daily Reflection

If I had to rate my day (1-10): _____

Did I achieve my top priorities today? If not, why not?

....

....

....

....

....

What lessons did I learn today that I can use to make tomorrow a better day?

....

....

....

....

....

....

What am I proud of today?

....

....

....

....

Daily Preparation

Goal Review:

....

....

....

"True freedom is impossible without a mind made free by discipline."
- Mortimer J. Adler

My ABCDE List

A-Tasks:

1. ....

2. ....

3. ....

B-Tasks:

1. ....

2. ....

3. ....

C-Tasks:

1. ....

2. ....

3. ....

D-Tasks:

1. ....

2. ....

3. ....

E-Tasks:

1. ....

2. ....

3. ....

My Daily Schedule

05:00
05:30
06:00
06:30
07:00
07:30
08:00
08:30
09:00
09:30
10:00
10:30
11:00
11:30
12:00
12:30
13:00

Notes:

....
....
....
....
....
....

| 13:30 |
| 14:00 |
| 14:30 |
| 15:00 |
| 15:30 |
| 16:00 |
| 16:30 |
| 17:00 |
| 17:30 |
| 18:00 |
| 18:30 |
| 19:00 |
| 19:30 |
| 20:00 |
| 20:30 |
| 21:00 |
| 21:30 |

Daily Reflection

If I had to rate my day (1–10): _____

Did I achieve my top priorities today? If not, why not?

....
....
....
....
....

What lessons did I learn today that I can use to make tomorrow a better day?

....
....
....
....
....

What am I proud of today?

....
....
....
....

Daily Preparation

Goal Review:

....

....

....

"The same level of thinking that created the problem won't solve the problem."
- Albert Einstein

My ABCDE List

A-Tasks:

1. ....

2. ....

3. ....

B-Tasks:

1. ....

2. ....

3. ....

C-Tasks:

1. ....

2. ....

3. ....

D-Tasks:

1. ....

2. ....

3. ....

E-Tasks:

1. ....

2. ....

3. ....

My Daily Schedule

05:00
05:30
06:00
06:30
07:00
07:30
08:00
08:30
09:00
09:30
10:00
10:30
11:00
11:30
12:00
12:30
13:00

Notes:

....

....

....

....

....

....

| 13:30 |
| 14:00 |
| 14:30 |
| 15:00 |
| 15:30 |
| 16:00 |
| 16:30 |
| 17:00 |
| 17:30 |
| 18:00 |
| 18:30 |
| 19:00 |
| 19:30 |
| 20:00 |
| 20:30 |
| 21:00 |
| 21:30 |

Daily Reflection

If I had to rate my day (1–10): _____

Did I achieve my top priorities today? If not, why not?

....

....

....

....

....

....

What lessons did I learn today that I can use to make tomorrow a better day?

....

....

....

....

....

What am I proud of today?

....

....

....

....

Daily Preparation

Goal Review:

....

....

....

My ABCDE List

My Daily Schedule

A-Tasks:

1. ....

2. ....

3. ....

B-Tasks:

1. ....

2. ....

3. ....

C-Tasks:

1. ....

2. ....

3. ....

D-Tasks:

1. ....

2. ....

3. ....

E-Tasks:

1. ....

2. ....

3. ....

Time
05:00
05:30
06:00
06:30
07:00
07:30
08:00
08:30
09:00
09:30
10:00
10:30
11:00
11:30
12:00
12:30
13:00

Notes:

....

....

....

....

....

....

13:30
14:00
14:30
15:00
15:30
16:00
16:30
17:00
17:30
18:00
18:30
19:00
19:30
20:00
20:30
21:00
21:30

Daily Reflection

If I had to rate my day (1-10): _____

Did I achieve my top priorities today? If not, why not?

....

....

....

....

....

....

What lessons did I learn today that I can use to make tomorrow a better day?

....

....

....

....

....

What am I proud of today?

....

....

....

....

Weekly Reflection

Did I achieve my top 3 goals of the week? If not, why not?

....

....

....

....

....

What lessons did I learn this week that I can use to make next week better?

....

....

....

....

....

What am I proud of this week?

....

....

....

....

Notes:

....

....

....

1st WEEK DOWN

You've made a great start!

Planner Progress

10%

9 WEEKS TO GO

Go rock that 2nd week!

"If you're brave enough to start, you're strong enough to finish"
- Gary R. Blair

Weekly Preparation

My top 3 goals of this week are:

1. ....

2. ....

3. ....

Weekly Schedule

Monday	Tuesday	Wednesday

Thursday	Friday	Weekend

Habit Tracker

	Mo	Tu	We	Th	Fr	Sa	Su
	☐	☐	☐	☐	☐	☐	☐
	☐	☐	☐	☐	☐	☐	☐
	☐	☐	☐	☐	☐	☐	☐
	☐	☐	☐	☐	☐	☐	☐
	☐	☐	☐	☐	☐	☐	☐

Daily Preparation

Goal Review:

....

....

....

My ABCDE List

A-Tasks:

1. ....

2. ....

3. ....

B-Tasks:

1. ....

2. ....

3. ....

C-Tasks:

1. ....

2. ....

3. ....

D-Tasks:

1. ....

2. ....

3. ....

E-Tasks:

1. ....

2. ....

3. ....

My Daily Schedule

Time
05:00
05:30
06:00
06:30
07:00
07:30
08:00
08:30
09:00
09:30
10:00
10:30
11:00
11:30
12:00
12:30
13:00

Notes:

....

....

....

....

....

| 13:30 |
| 14:00 |
| 14:30 |
| 15:00 |
| 15:30 |
| 16:00 |
| 16:30 |
| 17:00 |
| 17:30 |
| 18:00 |
| 18:30 |
| 19:00 |
| 19:30 |
| 20:00 |
| 20:30 |
| 21:00 |
| 21:30 |

Daily Reflection

If I had to rate my day (1-10): _____

Did I achieve my top priorities today? If not, why not?

....

....

....

....

....

....

What lessons did I learn today that I can use to make tomorrow a better day?

....

....

....

....

....

....

What am I proud of today?

....

....

....

....

Daily Preparation

Goal Review:

....

....

....

> "What we choose to focus on and what we choose to ignore—plays in defining the quality of our life."
> - Cal Newport

My ABCDE List

A-Tasks:

1. ....

2. ....

3. ....

B-Tasks:

1. ....

2. ....

3. ....

C-Tasks:

1. ....

2. ....

3. ....

D-Tasks:

1. ....

2. ....

3. ....

E-Tasks:

1. ....

2. ....

3. ....

My Daily Schedule

05:00	
05:30	
06:00	
06:30	
07:00	
07:30	
08:00	
08:30	
09:00	
09:30	
10:00	
10:30	
11:00	
11:30	
12:00	
12:30	
13:00	

Notes:

....

....

....

....

....

....

| 13:30 |
| 14:00 |
| 14:30 |
| 15:00 |
| 15:30 |
| 16:00 |
| 16:30 |
| 17:00 |
| 17:30 |
| 18:00 |
| 18:30 |
| 19:00 |
| 19:30 |
| 20:00 |
| 20:30 |
| 21:00 |
| 21:30 |

Daily Reflection

If I had to rate my day (1-10): _____

Did I achieve my top priorities today? If not, why not?

....

....

....

....

....

What lessons did I learn today that I can use to make tomorrow a better day?

....

....

....

....

....

....

What am I proud of today?

....

....

....

....

Daily Preparation

Goal Review:

....

....

....

My ABCDE List

A-Tasks:

1. ....
2. ....
3. ....

B-Tasks:

1. ....
2. ....
3. ....

C-Tasks:

1. ....
2. ....
3. ....

D-Tasks:

1. ....
2. ....
3. ....

E-Tasks:

1. ....
2. ....
3. ....

My Daily Schedule

Time
05:00
05:30
06:00
06:30
07:00
07:30
08:00
08:30
09:00
09:30
10:00
10:30
11:00
11:30
12:00
12:30
13:00

Notes:

....
....
....
....
....
....

| 13:30 |
| 14:00 |
| 14:30 |
| 15:00 |
| 15:30 |
| 16:00 |
| 16:30 |
| 17:00 |
| 17:30 |
| 18:00 |
| 18:30 |
| 19:00 |
| 19:30 |
| 20:00 |
| 20:30 |
| 21:00 |
| 21:30 |

Daily Reflection

If I had to rate my day (1–10): _____

Did I achieve my top priorities today? If not, why not?

....
....
....
....
....
....

What lessons did I learn today that I can use to make tomorrow a better day?

....
....
....
....
....

What am I proud of today?

....
....
....
....

Daily Preparation

Goal Review:

....

....

....

"You've got to wake up every morning with determination if you're going to go to bed with satisfaction."
- George Lorimer

My ABCDE List

A-Tasks:

1. ....

2. ....

3. ....

B-Tasks:

1. ....

2. ....

3. ....

C-Tasks:

1. ....

2. ....

3. ....

D-Tasks:

1. ....

2. ....

3. ....

E-Tasks:

1. ....

2. ....

3. ....

My Daily Schedule

05:00
05:30
06:00
06:30
07:00
07:30
08:00
08:30
09:00
09:30
10:00
10:30
11:00
11:30
12:00
12:30
13:00

Notes:	**Daily Reflection**
....	If I had to rate my day (1-10): _____
....	
....	Did I achieve my top priorities today? If not, why not?
....	....
....	....
....	....

13:30	....
14:00	....
14:30	....
15:00	What lessons did I learn today that I can use to make tomorrow a better day?
15:30	
16:00	....
16:30	....
17:00	....
17:30	....
18:00	....
18:30	....
19:00	....
19:30	What am I proud of today?
20:00	....
20:30	....
21:00	....
21:30	....

Daily Preparation

Goal Review:

....

....

....

"Great acts are made up of small deeds."
- Lao Tzu

My ABCDE List

A-Tasks:

1. ....

2. ....

3. ....

B-Tasks:

1. ....

2. ....

3. ....

C-Tasks:

1. ....

2. ....

3. ....

D-Tasks:

1. ....

2. ....

3. ....

E-Tasks:

1. ....

2. ....

3. ....

My Daily Schedule

05:00
05:30
06:00
06:30
07:00
07:30
08:00
08:30
09:00
09:30
10:00
10:30
11:00
11:30
12:00
12:30
13:00

Notes:

....

....

....

....

....

....

13:30
14:00
14:30
15:00
15:30
16:00
16:30
17:00
17:30
18:00
18:30
19:00
19:30
20:00
20:30
21:00
21:30

Daily Reflection

If I had to rate my day (1–10): _____

Did I achieve my top priorities today? If not, why not?

....

....

....

....

....

....

What lessons did I learn today that I can use to make tomorrow a better day?

....

....

....

....

....

....

What am I proud of today?

....

....

....

....

Daily Preparation

Today's Date: ___ /___ /___

Goal Review:

....

....

....

My ABCDE List

A-Tasks:

1. ....

2. ....

3. ....

B-Tasks:

1. ....

2. ....

3. ....

C-Tasks:

1. ....

2. ....

3. ....

D-Tasks:

1. ....

2. ....

3. ....

E-Tasks:

1. ....

2. ....

3. ....

My Daily Schedule

Time
05:00
05:30
06:00
06:30
07:00
07:30
08:00
08:30
09:00
09:30
10:00
10:30
11:00
11:30
12:00
12:30
13:00

Notes:

....

....

....

....

....

....

13:30	
14:00	
14:30	
15:00	
15:30	
16:00	
16:30	
17:00	
17:30	
18:00	
18:30	
19:00	
19:30	
20:00	
20:30	
21:00	
21:30	

Daily Reflection

If I had to rate my day (1-10): _____

Did I achieve my top priorities today? If not, why not?

....

....

....

....

....

....

What lessons did I learn today that I can use to make tomorrow a better day?

....

....

....

....

....

....

What am I proud of today?

....

....

....

....

Daily Preparation

Goal Review:

....

....

....

"To become a high performer requires thinking more before acting."
– Brendon Burchard

My ABCDE List

A-Tasks:

1. ....

2. ....

3. ....

B-Tasks:

1. ....

2. ....

3. ....

C-Tasks:

1. ....

2. ....

3. ....

D-Tasks:

1. ....

2. ....

3. ....

E-Tasks:

1. ....

2. ....

3. ....

My Daily Schedule

| 05:00 |
| 05:30 |
| 06:00 |
| 06:30 |
| 07:00 |
| 07:30 |
| 08:00 |
| 08:30 |
| 09:00 |
| 09:30 |
| 10:00 |
| 10:30 |
| 11:00 |
| 11:30 |
| 12:00 |
| 12:30 |
| 13:00 |

Notes:

....

....

....

....

....

....

13:30	
14:00	
14:30	
15:00	
15:30	
16:00	
16:30	
17:00	
17:30	
18:00	
18:30	
19:00	
19:30	
20:00	
20:30	
21:00	
21:30	

Daily Reflection

If I had to rate my day (1–10): _____

Did I achieve my top priorities today? If not, why not?

....

....

....

....

....

What lessons did I learn today that I can use to make tomorrow a better day?

....

....

....

....

....

....

What am I proud of today?

....

....

....

....

Weekly Reflection

Did I achieve my top 3 goals of the week? If not, why not?

....

....

....

....

....

What lessons did I learn this week that I can use to make next week better?

....

....

....

....

....

What am I proud of this week?

....

....

....

....

Notes:

....

....

....

2 WEEKS DOWN

Awesome work!

Planner Progress

20%

8 WEEKS TO GO

You're gaining momentum!

"Success is like a snowball. You gotta get it moving and the more you roll in the right direction the greater it gets."
– Steve Ferrante

Weekly Preparation

My top 3 goals of this week are:

1. ....

2. ....

3. ....

Weekly Schedule

Monday	Tuesday	Wednesday
Thursday	**Friday**	**Weekend**

Habit Tracker	Mo	Tu	We	Th	Fr	Sa	Su
	☐	☐	☐	☐	☐	☐	☐
	☐	☐	☐	☐	☐	☐	☐
	☐	☐	☐	☐	☐	☐	☐
	☐	☐	☐	☐	☐	☐	☐
	☐	☐	☐	☐	☐	☐	☐

Daily Preparation

Today's Date: ___ /___ /___

Goal Review:

....

....

....

My ABCDE List

A-Tasks:

1. ....
2. ....
3. ....

B-Tasks:

1. ....
2. ....
3. ....

C-Tasks:

1. ....
2. ....
3. ....

D-Tasks:

1. ....
2. ....
3. ....

E-Tasks:

1. ....
2. ....
3. ....

My Daily Schedule

Time
05:00
05:30
06:00
06:30
07:00
07:30
08:00
08:30
09:00
09:30
10:00
10:30
11:00
11:30
12:00
12:30
13:00

Notes:

....

....

....

....

....

....

| 13:30 |
| 14:00 |
| 14:30 |
| 15:00 |
| 15:30 |
| 16:00 |
| 16:30 |
| 17:00 |
| 17:30 |
| 18:00 |
| 18:30 |
| 19:00 |
| 19:30 |
| 20:00 |
| 20:30 |
| 21:00 |
| 21:30 |

Daily Reflection

If I had to rate my day (1–10): _____

Did I achieve my top priorities today? If not, why not?

....

....

....

....

....

....

What lessons did I learn today that I can use to make tomorrow a better day?

....

....

....

....

....

....

What am I proud of today?

....

....

....

....

Daily Preparation

Today's Date: ___ /___ /___

Goal Review:

....

....

....

"Greatness isn't born, it's grown."
- Daniel Coyle

My ABCDE List

A-Tasks:

1. ....
2. ....
3. ....

B-Tasks:

1. ....
2. ....
3. ....

C-Tasks:

1. ....
2. ....
3. ....

D-Tasks:

1. ....
2. ....
3. ....

E-Tasks:

1. ....
2. ....
3. ....

My Daily Schedule

Time
05:00
05:30
06:00
06:30
07:00
07:30
08:00
08:30
09:00
09:30
10:00
10:30
11:00
11:30
12:00
12:30
13:00

Notes:

....

....

....

....

....

....

13:30	
14:00	
14:30	
15:00	
15:30	
16:00	
16:30	
17:00	
17:30	
18:00	
18:30	
19:00	
19:30	
20:00	
20:30	
21:00	
21:30	

Daily Reflection

If I had to rate my day (1-10): _____

Did I achieve my top priorities today? If not, why not?

....

....

....

....

....

What lessons did I learn today that I can use to make tomorrow a better day?

....

....

....

....

....

....

What am I proud of today?

....

....

....

Daily Preparation

Goal Review:

....

....

....

"We do not need magic to transform our world. We carry all of the power we need inside ourselves already."
- J.K. Rowling

My ABCDE List

A-Tasks:

1. ....

2. ....

3. ....

B-Tasks:

1. ....

2. ....

3. ....

C-Tasks:

1. ....

2. ....

3. ....

D-Tasks:

1. ....

2. ....

3. ....

E-Tasks:

1. ....

2. ....

3. ....

My Daily Schedule

Time
05:00
05:30
06:00
06:30
07:00
07:30
08:00
08:30
09:00
09:30
10:00
10:30
11:00
11:30
12:00
12:30
13:00

Notes:

....

....

....

....

....

....

| 13:30 |
| 14:00 |
| 14:30 |
| 15:00 |
| 15:30 |
| 16:00 |
| 16:30 |
| 17:00 |
| 17:30 |
| 18:00 |
| 18:30 |
| 19:00 |
| 19:30 |
| 20:00 |
| 20:30 |
| 21:00 |
| 21:30 |

Daily Reflection

If I had to rate my day (1–10): _____

Did I achieve my top priorities today? If not, why not?

....

....

....

....

....

....

What lessons did I learn today that I can use to make tomorrow a better day?

....

....

....

....

....

....

What am I proud of today?

....

....

....

....

Daily Preparation

Goal Review:

....

....

....

*"Life has no limitations,
except the ones you make."*
- Les Brown

My ABCDE List

A-Tasks:

1. ....
2. ....
3. ....

B-Tasks:

1. ....
2. ....
3. ....

C-Tasks:

1. ....
2. ....
3. ....

D-Tasks:

1. ....
2. ....
3. ....

E-Tasks:

1. ....
2. ....
3. ....

My Daily Schedule

Time
05:00
05:30
06:00
06:30
07:00
07:30
08:00
08:30
09:00
09:30
10:00
10:30
11:00
11:30
12:00
12:30
13:00

Notes:

·······································
·······································
·······································
·······································
·······································
·······································

Time	
13:30	
14:00	
14:30	
15:00	
15:30	
16:00	
16:30	
17:00	
17:30	
18:00	
18:30	
19:00	
19:30	
20:00	
20:30	
21:00	
21:30	

Daily Reflection

If I had to rate my day (1-10): ____

Did I achieve my top priorities today? If not, why not?

·······································
·······································
·······································
·······································
·······································
·······································

What lessons did I learn today that I can use to make tomorrow a better day?

·······································
·······································
·······································
·······································
·······································
·······································

What am I proud of today?

·······································
·······································
·······································
·······································

Daily Preparation

Goal Review:

....

....

....

My ABCDE List

A-Tasks:

1. ....

2. ....

3. ....

B-Tasks:

1. ....

2. ....

3. ....

C-Tasks:

1. ....

2. ....

3. ....

D-Tasks:

1. ....

2. ....

3. ....

E-Tasks:

1. ....

2. ....

3. ....

My Daily Schedule

05:00	
05:30	
06:00	
06:30	
07:00	
07:30	
08:00	
08:30	
09:00	
09:30	
10:00	
10:30	
11:00	
11:30	
12:00	
12:30	
13:00	

Notes:

....

....

....

....

....

....

13:30	
14:00	
14:30	
15:00	
15:30	
16:00	
16:30	
17:00	
17:30	
18:00	
18:30	
19:00	
19:30	
20:00	
20:30	
21:00	
21:30	

Daily Reflection

If I had to rate my day (1–10): _____

Did I achieve my top priorities today? If not, why not?

....

....

....

....

....

What lessons did I learn today that I can use to make tomorrow a better day?

....

....

....

....

....

What am I proud of today?

....

....

....

....

Daily Preparation

Goal Review:

....

....

....

*"We first make our habits,
and then our habits make us."
– John Dryden*

My ABCDE List

A-Tasks:

1. ....
2. ....
3. ....

B-Tasks:

1. ....
2. ....
3. ....

C-Tasks:

1. ....
2. ....
3. ....

D-Tasks:

1. ....
2. ....
3. ....

E-Tasks:

1. ....
2. ....
3. ....

My Daily Schedule

Time
05:00
05:30
06:00
06:30
07:00
07:30
08:00
08:30
09:00
09:30
10:00
10:30
11:00
11:30
12:00
12:30
13:00

Notes:

....

....

....

....

....

....

13:30	
14:00	
14:30	
15:00	
15:30	
16:00	
16:30	
17:00	
17:30	
18:00	
18:30	
19:00	
19:30	
20:00	
20:30	
21:00	
21:30	

Daily Reflection

If I had to rate my day (1-10): _____

Did I achieve my top priorities today? If not, why not?

....

....

....

....

....

....

What lessons did I learn today that I can use to make tomorrow a better day?

....

....

....

....

....

....

What am I proud of today?

....

....

....

....

Daily Preparation

Goal Review:

....

....

....

"Habit is either the best of servants or the worst of masters."
- Nathaniel Emmons

My ABCDE List

A-Tasks:

1. ....
2. ....
3. ....

B-Tasks:

1. ....
2. ....
3. ....

C-Tasks:

1. ....
2. ....
3. ....

D-Tasks:

1. ....
2. ....
3. ....

E-Tasks:

1. ....
2. ....
3. ....

My Daily Schedule

05:00
05:30
06:00
06:30
07:00
07:30
08:00
08:30
09:00
09:30
10:00
10:30
11:00
11:30
12:00
12:30
13:00

Notes:

....

....

....

....

....

....

13:30	
14:00	
14:30	
15:00	
15:30	
16:00	
16:30	
17:00	
17:30	
18:00	
18:30	
19:00	
19:30	
20:00	
20:30	
21:00	
21:30	

Daily Reflection

If I had to rate my day (1-10): _____

Did I achieve my top priorities today? If not, why not?

....

....

....

....

....

What lessons did I learn today that I can use to make tomorrow a better day?

....

....

....

....

....

What am I proud of today?

....

....

....

....

Weekly Reflection

Did I achieve my top 3 goals of the week? If not, why not?

....

....

....

....

....

What lessons did I learn this week that I can use to make next week better?

....

....

....

....

....

What am I proud of this week?

....

....

....

....

Notes:

....

....

....

3 WEEKS DOWN

Amazing progress!

Planner Progress

30%

7 WEEKS TO GO

Keep it up!

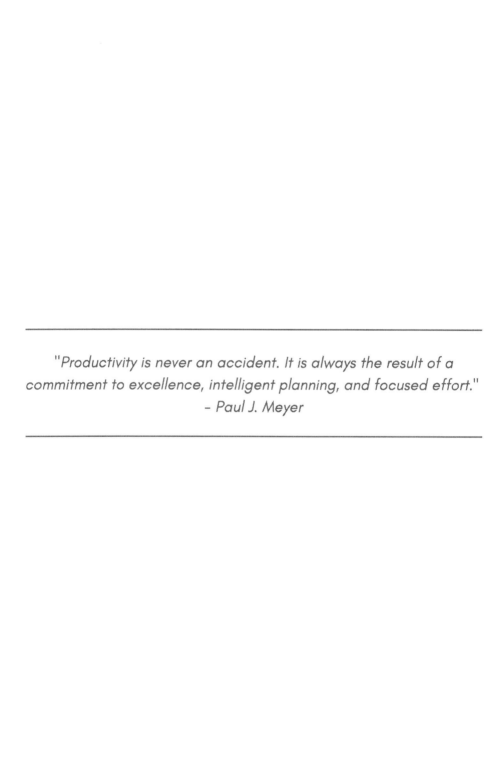

"*Productivity is never an accident. It is always the result of a commitment to excellence, intelligent planning, and focused effort.*"
- Paul J. Meyer

Weekly Preparation

My top 3 goals of this week are:

1. ....

2. ....

3. ....

Weekly Schedule

Monday	Tuesday	Wednesday

Thursday	Friday	Weekend

Habit Tracker	Mo	Tu	We	Th	Fr	Sa	Su
	☐	☐	☐	☐	☐	☐	☐
	☐	☐	☐	☐	☐	☐	☐
	☐	☐	☐	☐	☐	☐	☐
	☐	☐	☐	☐	☐	☐	☐
	☐	☐	☐	☐	☐	☐	☐

Daily Preparation

Goal Review:

....

....

....

"Nothing has such a power to broaden the mind as the ability to investigate systematically."
- Marcus Aurelius

My ABCDE List

A-Tasks:

1. ....

2. ....

3. ....

B-Tasks:

1. ....

2. ....

3. ....

C-Tasks:

1. ....

2. ....

3. ....

D-Tasks:

1. ....

2. ....

3. ....

E-Tasks:

1. ....

2. ....

3. ....

My Daily Schedule

Time
05:00
05:30
06:00
06:30
07:00
07:30
08:00
08:30
09:00
09:30
10:00
10:30
11:00
11:30
12:00
12:30
13:00

Notes:

....

....

....

....

....

....

| 13:30 |
| 14:00 |
| 14:30 |
| 15:00 |
| 15:30 |
| 16:00 |
| 16:30 |
| 17:00 |
| 17:30 |
| 18:00 |
| 18:30 |
| 19:00 |
| 19:30 |
| 20:00 |
| 20:30 |
| 21:00 |
| 21:30 |

Daily Reflection

If I had to rate my day (1–10): _____

Did I achieve my top priorities today? If not, why not?

....

....

....

....

....

....

What lessons did I learn today that I can use to make tomorrow a better day?

....

....

....

....

....

What am I proud of today?

....

....

....

....

Daily Preparation

Today's Date: ___ / ___ / ___

Goal Review:

....

....

....

My ABCDE List

A-Tasks:

1. ....
2. ....
3. ....

B-Tasks:

1. ....
2. ....
3. ....

C-Tasks:

1. ....
2. ....
3. ....

D-Tasks:

1. ....
2. ....
3. ....

E-Tasks:

1. ....
2. ....
3. ....

My Daily Schedule

Time
05:00
05:30
06:00
06:30
07:00
07:30
08:00
08:30
09:00
09:30
10:00
10:30
11:00
11:30
12:00
12:30
13:00

Notes:

....

....

....

....

....

....

| 13:30 |
| 14:00 |
| 14:30 |
| 15:00 |
| 15:30 |
| 16:00 |
| 16:30 |
| 17:00 |
| 17:30 |
| 18:00 |
| 18:30 |
| 19:00 |
| 19:30 |
| 20:00 |
| 20:30 |
| 21:00 |
| 21:30 |

Daily Reflection

If I had to rate my day (1-10): _____

Did I achieve my top priorities today? If not, why not?

....

....

....

....

....

....

What lessons did I learn today that I can use to make tomorrow a better day?

....

....

....

....

....

What am I proud of today?

....

....

....

....

Daily Preparation

Goal Review:

....

....

....

"The life which is unexamined is not worth living."
- Plato

My ABCDE List

A-Tasks:

1. ....
2. ....
3. ....

B-Tasks:

1. ....
2. ....
3. ....

C-Tasks:

1. ....
2. ....
3. ....

D-Tasks:

1. ....
2. ....
3. ....

E-Tasks:

1. ....
2. ....
3. ....

My Daily Schedule

05:00
05:30
06:00
06:30
07:00
07:30
08:00
08:30
09:00
09:30
10:00
10:30
11:00
11:30
12:00
12:30
13:00

Notes:

....

....

....

....

....

....

13:30
14:00
14:30
15:00
15:30
16:00
16:30
17:00
17:30
18:00
18:30
19:00
19:30
20:00
20:30
21:00
21:30

Daily Reflection

If I had to rate my day (1-10): _____

Did I achieve my top priorities today? If not, why not?

....

....

....

....

....

....

What lessons did I learn today that I can use to make tomorrow a better day?

....

....

....

....

....

....

What am I proud of today?

....

....

....

....

Daily Preparation

Goal Review:

....

....

....

My ABCDE List

A-Tasks:

1. ....

2. ....

3. ....

B-Tasks:

1. ....

2. ....

3. ....

C-Tasks:

1. ....

2. ....

3. ....

D-Tasks:

1. ....

2. ....

3. ....

E-Tasks:

1. ....

2. ....

3. ....

My Daily Schedule

05:00
05:30
06:00
06:30
07:00
07:30
08:00
08:30
09:00
09:30
10:00
10:30
11:00
11:30
12:00
12:30
13:00

Notes:

....

....

....

....

....

....

13:30	
14:00	
14:30	
15:00	
15:30	
16:00	
16:30	
17:00	
17:30	
18:00	
18:30	
19:00	
19:30	
20:00	
20:30	
21:00	
21:30	

Daily Reflection

If I had to rate my day (1–10): _____

Did I achieve my top priorities today? If not, why not?

....

....

....

....

....

What lessons did I learn today that I can use to make tomorrow a better day?

....

....

....

....

....

What am I proud of today?

....

....

....

....

Daily Preparation

Today's Date: ___ /___ /___

Goal Review:

....

....

....

My ABCDE List

A-Tasks:

1. ....

2. ....

3. ....

B-Tasks:

1. ....

2. ....

3. ....

C-Tasks:

1. ....

2. ....

3. ....

D-Tasks:

1. ....

2. ....

3. ....

E-Tasks:

1. ....

2. ....

3. ....

My Daily Schedule

Time
05:00
05:30
06:00
06:30
07:00
07:30
08:00
08:30
09:00
09:30
10:00
10:30
11:00
11:30
12:00
12:30
13:00

Notes:

....

....

....

....

....

....

13:30
14:00
14:30
15:00
15:30
16:00
16:30
17:00
17:30
18:00
18:30
19:00
19:30
20:00
20:30
21:00
21:30

Daily Reflection

If I had to rate my day (1-10): _____

Did I achieve my top priorities today? If not, why not?

....

....

....

....

....

....

What lessons did I learn today that I can use to make tomorrow a better day?

....

....

....

....

....

....

What am I proud of today?

....

....

....

....

Daily Preparation

Today's Date: ___ / ___ / ___

Goal Review:

....

....

....

> *"A man is rich in proportion to the number of things he can afford to let alone."*
> – Henry David Thoreau

My ABCDE List

A-Tasks:

1. ....

2. ....

3. ....

B-Tasks:

1. ....

2. ....

3. ....

C-Tasks:

1. ....

2. ....

3. ....

D-Tasks:

1. ....

2. ....

3. ....

E-Tasks:

1. ....

2. ....

3. ....

My Daily Schedule

Time
05:00
05:30
06:00
06:30
07:00
07:30
08:00
08:30
09:00
09:30
10:00
10:30
11:00
11:30
12:00
12:30
13:00

Notes:

....

....

....

....

....

....

13:30	
14:00	
14:30	
15:00	
15:30	
16:00	
16:30	
17:00	
17:30	
18:00	
18:30	
19:00	
19:30	
20:00	
20:30	
21:00	
21:30	

Daily Reflection

If I had to rate my day (1–10): _____

Did I achieve my top priorities today? If not, why not?

....

....

....

....

....

....

What lessons did I learn today that I can use to make tomorrow a better day?

....

....

....

....

....

....

What am I proud of today?

....

....

....

....

Daily Preparation

Today's Date: ___ / ___ / ___

Goal Review:

....

....

....

My ABCDE List

A-Tasks:

1. ....

2. ....

3. ....

B-Tasks:

1. ....

2. ....

3. ....

C-Tasks:

1. ....

2. ....

3. ....

D-Tasks:

1. ....

2. ....

3. ....

E-Tasks:

1. ....

2. ....

3. ....

My Daily Schedule

Time
05:00
05:30
06:00
06:30
07:00
07:30
08:00
08:30
09:00
09:30
10:00
10:30
11:00
11:30
12:00
12:30
13:00

Notes:

....

....

....

....

....

....

| 13:30 |
| 14:00 |
| 14:30 |
| 15:00 |
| 15:30 |
| 16:00 |
| 16:30 |
| 17:00 |
| 17:30 |
| 18:00 |
| 18:30 |
| 19:00 |
| 19:30 |
| 20:00 |
| 20:30 |
| 21:00 |
| 21:30 |

Daily Reflection

If I had to rate my day (1-10): _____

Did I achieve my top priorities today? If not, why not?

....

....

....

....

....

What lessons did I learn today that I can use to make tomorrow a better day?

....

....

....

....

....

....

What am I proud of today?

....

....

....

....

Weekly Reflection

Did I achieve my top 3 goals of the week? If not, why not?

....

....

....

....

....

What lessons did I learn this week that I can use to make next week better?

....

....

....

....

....

What am I proud of this week?

....

....

....

....

Notes:

....

....

....

4 WEEKS DOWN

You're nearly halfway!

Planner Progress

40%

6 WEEKS TO GO

Stay focused!

"*Ambition is the path to success.*
Persistence is the vehicle you arrive in."
- Bill Bradley

Weekly Preparation

My top 3 goals of this week are:

1. ....

2. ....

3. ....

Weekly Schedule

Monday	Tuesday	Wednesday

Thursday	Friday	Weekend

Habit Tracker

	Mo	Tu	We	Th	Fr	Sa	Su
	☐	☐	☐	☐	☐	☐	☐
	☐	☐	☐	☐	☐	☐	☐
	☐	☐	☐	☐	☐	☐	☐
	☐	☐	☐	☐	☐	☐	☐
	☐	☐	☐	☐	☐	☐	☐

Daily Preparation

Goal Review:

....

....

....

"In theory there is no difference between theory and practice. But, in practice, there is."
- Jan van de Snepscheut

My ABCDE List

A-Tasks:

1. ....

2. ....

3. ....

B-Tasks:

1. ....

2. ....

3. ....

C-Tasks:

1. ....

2. ....

3. ....

D-Tasks:

1. ....

2. ....

3. ....

E-Tasks:

1. ....

2. ....

3. ....

My Daily Schedule

Time
05:00
05:30
06:00
06:30
07:00
07:30
08:00
08:30
09:00
09:30
10:00
10:30
11:00
11:30
12:00
12:30
13:00

Notes:

....

....

....

....

....

....

13:30	
14:00	
14:30	
15:00	
15:30	
16:00	
16:30	
17:00	
17:30	
18:00	
18:30	
19:00	
19:30	
20:00	
20:30	
21:00	
21:30	

Daily Reflection

If I had to rate my day (1-10): _____

Did I achieve my top priorities today? If not, why not?

....

....

....

....

....

....

What lessons did I learn today that I can use to make tomorrow a better day?

....

....

....

....

....

What am I proud of today?

....

....

....

....

Daily Preparation

Goal Review:

....

....

....

My ABCDE List

A-Tasks:

1. ....

2. ....

3. ....

B-Tasks:

1. ....

2. ....

3. ....

C-Tasks:

1. ....

2. ....

3. ....

D-Tasks:

1. ....

2. ....

3. ....

E-Tasks:

1. ....

2. ....

3. ....

My Daily Schedule

Time
05:00
05:30
06:00
06:30
07:00
07:30
08:00
08:30
09:00
09:30
10:00
10:30
11:00
11:30
12:00
12:30
13:00

Notes:

....

....

....

....

....

....

| 13:30 |
| 14:00 |
| 14:30 |
| 15:00 |
| 15:30 |
| 16:00 |
| 16:30 |
| 17:00 |
| 17:30 |
| 18:00 |
| 18:30 |
| 19:00 |
| 19:30 |
| 20:00 |
| 20:30 |
| 21:00 |
| 21:30 |

Daily Reflection

If I had to rate my day (1–10): _____

Did I achieve my top priorities today? If not, why not?

....

....

....

....

....

What lessons did I learn today that I can use to make tomorrow a better day?

....

....

....

....

....

What am I proud of today?

....

....

....

....

Daily Preparation

Goal Review:

....

....

....

"Do what you can, with what you have, where your are."
- Theodore Roosevelt

My ABCDE List

A-Tasks:

1. ....

2. ....

3. ....

B-Tasks:

1. ....

2. ....

3. ....

C-Tasks:

1. ....

2. ....

3. ....

D-Tasks:

1. ....

2. ....

3. ....

E-Tasks:

1. ....

2. ....

3. ....

My Daily Schedule

05:00
05:30
06:00
06:30
07:00
07:30
08:00
08:30
09:00
09:30
10:00
10:30
11:00
11:30
12:00
12:30
13:00

Notes:

....

....

....

....

....

....

13:30	
14:00	
14:30	
15:00	
15:30	
16:00	
16:30	
17:00	
17:30	
18:00	
18:30	
19:00	
19:30	
20:00	
20:30	
21:00	
21:30	

Daily Reflection

If I had to rate my day (1-10): _____

Did I achieve my top priorities today? If not, why not?

....

....

....

....

....

....

What lessons did I learn today that I can use to make tomorrow a better day?

....

....

....

....

....

....

What am I proud of today?

....

....

....

....

Daily Preparation

Today's Date: ___ / ___ / ___

Goal Review:

....

....

....

My ABCDE List

A-Tasks:

1. ....

2. ....

3. ....

B-Tasks:

1. ....

2. ....

3. ....

C-Tasks:

1. ....

2. ....

3. ....

D-Tasks:

1. ....

2. ....

3. ....

E-Tasks:

1. ....

2. ....

3. ....

My Daily Schedule

Time
05:00
05:30
06:00
06:30
07:00
07:30
08:00
08:30
09:00
09:30
10:00
10:30
11:00
11:30
12:00
12:30
13:00

Notes:

....

....

....

....

....

....

13:30	
14:00	
14:30	
15:00	
15:30	
16:00	
16:30	
17:00	
17:30	
18:00	
18:30	
19:00	
19:30	
20:00	
20:30	
21:00	
21:30	

Daily Reflection

If I had to rate my day (1–10): _____

Did I achieve my top priorities today? If not, why not?

....

....

....

....

....

....

What lessons did I learn today that I can use to make tomorrow a better day?

....

....

....

....

....

What am I proud of today?

....

....

....

....

Daily Preparation

Goal Review:

....

....

....

"There is nothing so useless as doing efficiently that which should not be done at all."
- Peter Drucker

My ABCDE List

A-Tasks:

1. ....

2. ....

3. ....

B-Tasks:

1. ....

2. ....

3. ....

C-Tasks:

1. ....

2. ....

3. ....

D-Tasks:

1. ....

2. ....

3. ....

E-Tasks:

1. ....

2. ....

3. ....

My Daily Schedule

Time
05:00
05:30
06:00
06:30
07:00
07:30
08:00
08:30
09:00
09:30
10:00
10:30
11:00
11:30
12:00
12:30
13:00

Notes:

....

....

....

....

....

....

13:30	
14:00	
14:30	
15:00	
15:30	
16:00	
16:30	
17:00	
17:30	
18:00	
18:30	
19:00	
19:30	
20:00	
20:30	
21:00	
21:30	

Daily Reflection

If I had to rate my day (1-10): _____

Did I achieve my top priorities today? If not, why not?

....

....

....

....

....

....

What lessons did I learn today that I can use to make tomorrow a better day?

....

....

....

....

....

....

What am I proud of today?

....

....

....

....

Daily Preparation

Today's Date: ___ /___ /___

Goal Review:

....

....

....

My ABCDE List

A-Tasks:

1. ....
2. ....
3. ....

B-Tasks:

1. ....
2. ....
3. ....

C-Tasks:

1. ....
2. ....
3. ....

D-Tasks:

1. ....
2. ....
3. ....

E-Tasks:

1. ....
2. ....
3. ....

My Daily Schedule

Time
05:00
05:30
06:00
06:30
07:00
07:30
08:00
08:30
09:00
09:30
10:00
10:30
11:00
11:30
12:00
12:30
13:00

Notes:

....

....

....

....

....

....

| 13:30 |
| 14:00 |
| 14:30 |
| 15:00 |
| 15:30 |
| 16:00 |
| 16:30 |
| 17:00 |
| 17:30 |
| 18:00 |
| 18:30 |
| 19:00 |
| 19:30 |
| 20:00 |
| 20:30 |
| 21:00 |
| 21:30 |

Daily Reflection

If I had to rate my day (1–10): _____

Did I achieve my top priorities today? If not, why not?

....

....

....

....

....

....

What lessons did I learn today that I can use to make tomorrow a better day?

....

....

....

....

....

....

What am I proud of today?

....

....

....

....

Daily Preparation

Today's Date: ___ /___ /___

Goal Review:

....

....

....

My ABCDE List

A-Tasks:

1. ....

2. ....

3. ....

B-Tasks:

1. ....

2. ....

3. ....

C-Tasks:

1. ....

2. ....

3. ....

D-Tasks:

1. ....

2. ....

3. ....

E-Tasks:

1. ....

2. ....

3. ....

My Daily Schedule

05:00	
05:30	
06:00	
06:30	
07:00	
07:30	
08:00	
08:30	
09:00	
09:30	
10:00	
10:30	
11:00	
11:30	
12:00	
12:30	
13:00	

Notes:

....

....

....

....

....

....

13:30
14:00
14:30
15:00
15:30
16:00
16:30
17:00
17:30
18:00
18:30
19:00
19:30
20:00
20:30
21:00
21:30

Daily Reflection

If I had to rate my day (1-10): _____

Did I achieve my top priorities today? If not, why not?

....

....

....

....

....

....

What lessons did I learn today that I can use to make tomorrow a better day?

....

....

....

....

....

....

What am I proud of today?

....

....

....

....

Weekly Reflection

Did I achieve my top 3 goals of the week? If not, why not?

....

....

....

....

....

What lessons did I learn this week that I can use to make next week better?

....

....

....

....

What am I proud of this week?

....

....

....

Notes:

....

....

....

5 WEEKS DOWN

You're halfway!

Planner Progress

50%

5 WEEKS TO GO

Make them count!

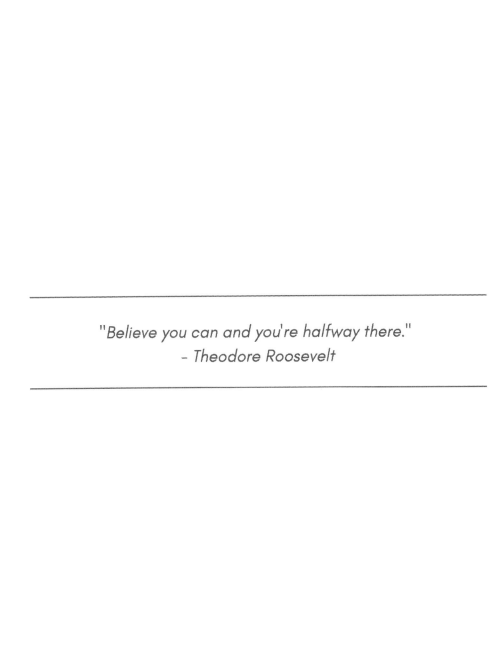

"Believe you can and you're halfway there."
- Theodore Roosevelt

Weekly Preparation

My top 3 goals of this week are:

1. ....

2. ....

3. ....

Weekly Schedule

Monday	Tuesday	Wednesday
Thursday	Friday	Weekend

Habit Tracker	Mo	Tu	We	Th	Fr	Sa	Su
	☐	☐	☐	☐	☐	☐	☐
	☐	☐	☐	☐	☐	☐	☐
	☐	☐	☐	☐	☐	☐	☐
	☐	☐	☐	☐	☐	☐	☐
	☐	☐	☐	☐	☐	☐	☐

Daily Preparation

Goal Review:

....

....

....

"If you don't make mistakes, you're not working on hard enough problems. And that's a big mistake."
- Frank Wilczek

My ABCDE List

A-Tasks:

1. ....

2. ....

3. ....

B-Tasks:

1. ....

2. ....

3. ....

C-Tasks:

1. ....

2. ....

3. ....

D-Tasks:

1. ....

2. ....

3. ....

E-Tasks:

1. ....

2. ....

3. ....

My Daily Schedule

Time
05:00
05:30
06:00
06:30
07:00
07:30
08:00
08:30
09:00
09:30
10:00
10:30
11:00
11:30
12:00
12:30
13:00

Notes:

....

....

....

....

....

| 13:30 |
| 14:00 |
| 14:30 |
| 15:00 |
| 15:30 |
| 16:00 |
| 16:30 |
| 17:00 |
| 17:30 |
| 18:00 |
| 18:30 |
| 19:00 |
| 19:30 |
| 20:00 |
| 20:30 |
| 21:00 |
| 21:30 |

Daily Reflection

If I had to rate my day (1-10): _____

Did I achieve my top priorities today? If not, why not?

....

....

....

....

....

....

What lessons did I learn today that I can use to make tomorrow a better day?

....

....

....

....

....

....

What am I proud of today?

....

....

....

....

Daily Preparation

Today's Date: ___ /___ /___

Goal Review:

....

....

....

"Dreams come true. You just have to be willing to work for them."
- Annie Mist

My ABCDE List

A-Tasks:

1. ....

2. ....

3. ....

B-Tasks:

1. ....

2. ....

3. ....

C-Tasks:

1. ....

2. ....

3. ....

D-Tasks:

1. ....

2. ....

3. ....

E-Tasks:

1. ....

2. ....

3. ....

My Daily Schedule

05:00
05:30
06:00
06:30
07:00
07:30
08:00
08:30
09:00
09:30
10:00
10:30
11:00
11:30
12:00
12:30
13:00

Notes:
....
....
....
....
....

13:30	
14:00	
14:30	
15:00	
15:30	
16:00	
16:30	
17:00	
17:30	
18:00	
18:30	
19:00	
19:30	
20:00	
20:30	
21:00	
21:30	

Daily Reflection

If I had to rate my day (1-10): _____

Did I achieve my top priorities today? If not, why not?

....
....
....
....
....

What lessons did I learn today that I can use to make tomorrow a better day?

....
....
....
....
....

What am I proud of today?

....
....
....
....

Daily Preparation

Goal Review:

....

....

....

"A schedule defends from chaos and whim. It is a net for catching days."
- Annie Dillard

My ABCDE List

A-Tasks:

1. ....

2. ....

3. ....

B-Tasks:

1. ....

2. ....

3. ....

C-Tasks:

1. ....

2. ....

3. ....

D-Tasks:

1. ....

2. ....

3. ....

E-Tasks:

1. ....

2. ....

3. ....

My Daily Schedule

Time
05:00
05:30
06:00
06:30
07:00
07:30
08:00
08:30
09:00
09:30
10:00
10:30
11:00
11:30
12:00
12:30
13:00

Notes:	**Daily Reflection**

Notes:

....

....

....

....

....

....

| 13:30 |
| 14:00 |
| 14:30 |
| 15:00 |
| 15:30 |
| 16:00 |
| 16:30 |
| 17:00 |
| 17:30 |
| 18:00 |
| 18:30 |
| 19:00 |
| 19:30 |
| 20:00 |
| 20:30 |
| 21:00 |
| 21:30 |

Daily Reflection

If I had to rate my day (1-10): _____

Did I achieve my top priorities today? If not, why not?

....

....

....

....

....

....

What lessons did I learn today that I can use to make tomorrow a better day?

....

....

....

....

....

What am I proud of today?

....

....

....

....

Daily Preparation

Today's Date: ___ /___ /___

Goal Review:

....

....

....

My ABCDE List

A-Tasks:

1. ....

2. ....

3. ....

B-Tasks:

1. ....

2. ....

3. ....

C-Tasks:

1. ....

2. ....

3. ....

D-Tasks:

1. ....

2. ....

3. ....

E-Tasks:

1. ....

2. ....

3. ....

My Daily Schedule

05:00
05:30
06:00
06:30
07:00
07:30
08:00
08:30
09:00
09:30
10:00
10:30
11:00
11:30
12:00
12:30
13:00

Notes:

....

....

....

....

....

| 13:30 |
| 14:00 |
| 14:30 |
| 15:00 |
| 15:30 |
| 16:00 |
| 16:30 |
| 17:00 |
| 17:30 |
| 18:00 |
| 18:30 |
| 19:00 |
| 19:30 |
| 20:00 |
| 20:30 |
| 21:00 |
| 21:30 |

Daily Reflection

If I had to rate my day (1–10): _____

Did I achieve my top priorities today? If not, why not?

....

....

....

....

....

What lessons did I learn today that I can use to make tomorrow a better day?

....

....

....

....

....

What am I proud of today?

....

....

....

....

Daily Preparation

Goal Review:

....

....

....

"Discipline equals freedom."
- Jocko Willink

My ABCDE List

A-Tasks:

1. ....

2. ....

3. ....

B-Tasks:

1. ....

2. ....

3. ....

C-Tasks:

1. ....

2. ....

3. ....

D-Tasks:

1. ....

2. ....

3. ....

E-Tasks:

1. ....

2. ....

3. ....

My Daily Schedule

Time
05:00
05:30
06:00
06:30
07:00
07:30
08:00
08:30
09:00
09:30
10:00
10:30
11:00
11:30
12:00
12:30
13:00

Notes:

....

....

....

....

....

13:30
14:00
14:30
15:00
15:30
16:00
16:30
17:00
17:30
18:00
18:30
19:00
19:30
20:00
20:30
21:00
21:30

Daily Reflection

If I had to rate my day (1-10): _____

Did I achieve my top priorities today? If not, why not?

....

....

....

....

....

What lessons did I learn today that I can use to make tomorrow a better day?

....

....

....

....

....

....

What am I proud of today?

....

....

....

....

Daily Preparation

Today's Date: ___ / ___ / ___

_____

Goal Review:

....

....

....

_____

My ABCDE List

A-Tasks:

1. ....

2. ....

3. ....

B-Tasks:

1. ....

2. ....

3. ....

C-Tasks:

1. ....

2. ....

3. ....

D-Tasks:

1. ....

2. ....

3. ....

E-Tasks:

1. ....

2. ....

3. ....

My Daily Schedule

Time
05:00
05:30
06:00
06:30
07:00
07:30
08:00
08:30
09:00
09:30
10:00
10:30
11:00
11:30
12:00
12:30
13:00

Notes:

....

....

....

....

....

....

Time
13:30
14:00
14:30
15:00
15:30
16:00
16:30
17:00
17:30
18:00
18:30
19:00
19:30
20:00
20:30
21:00
21:30

Daily Reflection

If I had to rate my day (1–10): _____

Did I achieve my top priorities today? If not, why not?

....

....

....

....

....

What lessons did I learn today that I can use to make tomorrow a better day?

....

....

....

....

....

....

What am I proud of today?

....

....

....

....

Daily Preparation

Today's Date: ___ /___ /___

Goal Review:

....

....

....

My ABCDE List

A-Tasks:

1. ....

2. ....

3. ....

B-Tasks:

1. ....

2. ....

3. ....

C-Tasks:

1. ....

2. ....

3. ....

D-Tasks:

1. ....

2. ....

3. ....

E-Tasks:

1. ....

2. ....

3. ....

My Daily Schedule

Time
05:00
05:30
06:00
06:30
07:00
07:30
08:00
08:30
09:00
09:30
10:00
10:30
11:00
11:30
12:00
12:30
13:00

Notes:

....

....

....

....

....

....

| 13:30 |
| 14:00 |
| 14:30 |
| 15:00 |
| 15:30 |
| 16:00 |
| 16:30 |
| 17:00 |
| 17:30 |
| 18:00 |
| 18:30 |
| 19:00 |
| 19:30 |
| 20:00 |
| 20:30 |
| 21:00 |
| 21:30 |

Daily Reflection

If I had to rate my day (1-10): _____

Did I achieve my top priorities today? If not, why not?

....

....

....

....

....

What lessons did I learn today that I can use to make tomorrow a better day?

....

....

....

....

....

What am I proud of today?

....

....

....

....

Weekly Reflection

Did I achieve my top 3 goals of the week? If not, why not?

....

....

....

....

....

What lessons did I learn this week that I can use to make next week better?

....

....

....

....

What am I proud of this week?

....

....

....

Notes:

....

....

....

6 WEEKS DOWN

That's amazing!

Planner Progress

60%

4 WEEKS TO GO

Keep it up!

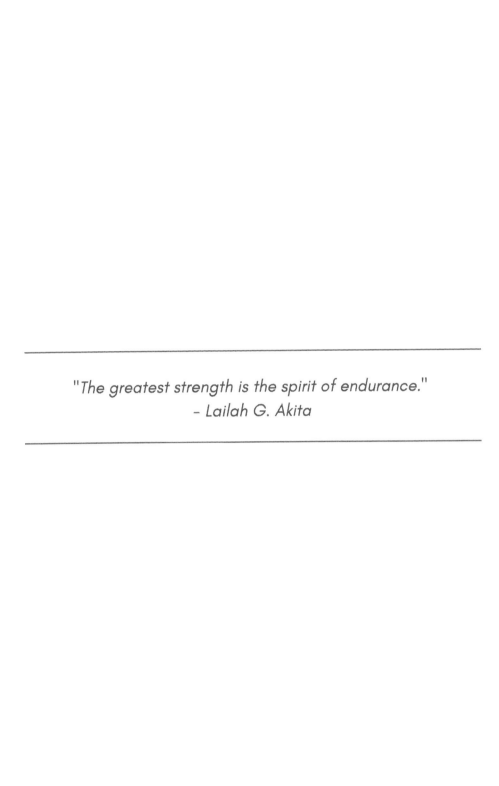

"*The greatest strength is the spirit of endurance.*"
- Lailah G. Akita

Weekly Preparation

My top 3 goals of this week are:

1. ....

2. ....

3. ....

Weekly Schedule

Monday	Tuesday	Wednesday
Thursday	Friday	Weekend

Habit Tracker	Mo	Tu	We	Th	Fr	Sa	Su
	☐	☐	☐	☐	☐	☐	☐
	☐	☐	☐	☐	☐	☐	☐
	☐	☐	☐	☐	☐	☐	☐
	☐	☐	☐	☐	☐	☐	☐
	☐	☐	☐	☐	☐	☐	☐

Daily Preparation

Today's Date: ___ / ___ / ___

Goal Review:

....

....

....

My ABCDE List

A-Tasks:

1. ....

2. ....

3. ....

B-Tasks:

1. ....

2. ....

3. ....

C-Tasks:

1. ....

2. ....

3. ....

D-Tasks:

1. ....

2. ....

3. ....

E-Tasks:

1. ....

2. ....

3. ....

My Daily Schedule

Time
05:00
05:30
06:00
06:30
07:00
07:30
08:00
08:30
09:00
09:30
10:00
10:30
11:00
11:30
12:00
12:30
13:00

Notes:

....

....

....

....

....

| 13:30 |
| 14:00 |
| 14:30 |
| 15:00 |
| 15:30 |
| 16:00 |
| 16:30 |
| 17:00 |
| 17:30 |
| 18:00 |
| 18:30 |
| 19:00 |
| 19:30 |
| 20:00 |
| 20:30 |
| 21:00 |
| 21:30 |

Daily Reflection

If I had to rate my day (1-10):
_____

Did I achieve my top priorities today? If not, why not?

....

....

....

....

....

What lessons did I learn today that I can use to make tomorrow a better day?

....

....

....

....

What am I proud of today?

....

....

....

....

Daily Preparation

Today's Date: ___ /___ /___

Goal Review:

....

....

....

My ABCDE List

A-Tasks:

1. ....

2. ....

3. ....

B-Tasks:

1. ....

2. ....

3. ....

C-Tasks:

1. ....

2. ....

3. ....

D-Tasks:

1. ....

2. ....

3. ....

E-Tasks:

1. ....

2. ....

3. ....

My Daily Schedule

Time
05:00
05:30
06:00
06:30
07:00
07:30
08:00
08:30
09:00
09:30
10:00
10:30
11:00
11:30
12:00
12:30
13:00

Notes:
....

....

....

....

....

13:30	
14:00	
14:30	
15:00	
15:30	
16:00	
16:30	
17:00	
17:30	
18:00	
18:30	
19:00	
19:30	
20:00	
20:30	
21:00	
21:30	

Daily Reflection

If I had to rate my day (1–10): _____

Did I achieve my top priorities today? If not, why not?

....

....

....

....

....

....

What lessons did I learn today that I can use to make tomorrow a better day?

....

....

....

....

....

....

What am I proud of today?

....

....

....

....

Daily Preparation

Goal Review:

....

....

....

My ABCDE List

A-Tasks:

1. ....
2. ....
3. ....

B-Tasks:

1. ....
2. ....
3. ....

C-Tasks:

1. ....
2. ....
3. ....

D-Tasks:

1. ....
2. ....
3. ....

E-Tasks:

1. ....
2. ....
3. ....

My Daily Schedule

05:00
05:30
06:00
06:30
07:00
07:30
08:00
08:30
09:00
09:30
10:00
10:30
11:00
11:30
12:00
12:30
13:00

Notes:

....

....

....

....

....

....

13:30
14:00
14:30
15:00
15:30
16:00
16:30
17:00
17:30
18:00
18:30
19:00
19:30
20:00
20:30
21:00
21:30

Daily Reflection

If I had to rate my day (1–10): _____

Did I achieve my top priorities today? If not, why not?

....

....

....

....

....

....

What lessons did I learn today that I can use to make tomorrow a better day?

....

....

....

....

....

....

What am I proud of today?

....

....

....

....

Daily Preparation

Today's Date: ___ /___ /___

Goal Review:

....

....

....

My ABCDE List

A-Tasks:

1. ....

2. ....

3. ....

B-Tasks:

1. ....

2. ....

3. ....

C-Tasks:

1. ....

2. ....

3. ....

D-Tasks:

1. ....

2. ....

3. ....

E-Tasks:

1. ....

2. ....

3. ....

My Daily Schedule

05:00
05:30
06:00
06:30
07:00
07:30
08:00
08:30
09:00
09:30
10:00
10:30
11:00
11:30
12:00
12:30
13:00

Notes:

....

....

....

....

....

....

| 13:30 |
| 14:00 |
| 14:30 |
| 15:00 |
| 15:30 |
| 16:00 |
| 16:30 |
| 17:00 |
| 17:30 |
| 18:00 |
| 18:30 |
| 19:00 |
| 19:30 |
| 20:00 |
| 20:30 |
| 21:00 |
| 21:30 |

Daily Reflection

If I had to rate my day (1-10): _____

Did I achieve my top priorities today? If not, why not?

....

....

....

....

....

What lessons did I learn today that I can use to make tomorrow a better day?

....

....

....

....

....

What am I proud of today?

....

....

....

....

Daily Preparation

Today's Date: ___ /___ /___

Goal Review:

....

....

....

My ABCDE List

A-Tasks:

1. ....

2. ....

3. ....

B-Tasks:

1. ....

2. ....

3. ....

C-Tasks:

1. ....

2. ....

3. ....

D-Tasks:

1. ....

2. ....

3. ....

E-Tasks:

1. ....

2. ....

3. ....

My Daily Schedule

Time
05:00
05:30
06:00
06:30
07:00
07:30
08:00
08:30
09:00
09:30
10:00
10:30
11:00
11:30
12:00
12:30
13:00

Notes:

....

....

....

....

....

| 13:30 |
| 14:00 |
| 14:30 |
| 15:00 |
| 15:30 |
| 16:00 |
| 16:30 |
| 17:00 |
| 17:30 |
| 18:00 |
| 18:30 |
| 19:00 |
| 19:30 |
| 20:00 |
| 20:30 |
| 21:00 |
| 21:30 |

Daily Reflection

If I had to rate my day (1-10): _____

Did I achieve my top priorities today? If not, why not?

....

....

....

....

....

What lessons did I learn today that I can use to make tomorrow a better day?

....

....

....

....

....

What am I proud of today?

....

....

....

....

Daily Preparation

Today's Date: ___ /___ /___

Goal Review:

....

....

....

My ABCDE List

A-Tasks:

1. ....

2. ....

3. ....

B-Tasks:

1. ....

2. ....

3. ....

C-Tasks:

1. ....

2. ....

3. ....

D-Tasks:

1. ....

2. ....

3. ....

E-Tasks:

1. ....

2. ....

3. ....

My Daily Schedule

Time
05:00
05:30
06:00
06:30
07:00
07:30
08:00
08:30
09:00
09:30
10:00
10:30
11:00
11:30
12:00
12:30
13:00

Notes:

....

....

....

....

....

....

13:30	
14:00	
14:30	
15:00	
15:30	
16:00	
16:30	
17:00	
17:30	
18:00	
18:30	
19:00	
19:30	
20:00	
20:30	
21:00	
21:30	

Daily Reflection

If I had to rate my day (1-10): _____

Did I achieve my top priorities today? If not, why not?

....

....

....

....

....

What lessons did I learn today that I can use to make tomorrow a better day?

....

....

....

....

....

What am I proud of today?

....

....

....

....

Daily Preparation

Today's Date: ___ / ___ / ___

Goal Review:

....

....

....

My ABCDE List

My Daily Schedule

A-Tasks:

1. ....

2. ....

3. ....

B-Tasks:

1. ....

2. ....

3. ....

C-Tasks:

1. ....

2. ....

3. ....

D-Tasks:

1. ....

2. ....

3. ....

E-Tasks:

1. ....

2. ....

3. ....

My Daily Schedule
05:00
05:30
06:00
06:30
07:00
07:30
08:00
08:30
09:00
09:30
10:00
10:30
11:00
11:30
12:00
12:30
13:00

Notes:

....

....

....

....

....

....

| 13:30 |
| 14:00 |
| 14:30 |
| 15:00 |
| 15:30 |
| 16:00 |
| 16:30 |
| 17:00 |
| 17:30 |
| 18:00 |
| 18:30 |
| 19:00 |
| 19:30 |
| 20:00 |
| 20:30 |
| 21:00 |
| 21:30 |

Daily Reflection

If I had to rate my day (1-10): _____

Did I achieve my top priorities today? If not, why not?

....

....

....

....

....

....

What lessons did I learn today that I can use to make tomorrow a better day?

....

....

....

....

....

What am I proud of today?

....

....

....

....

Weekly Reflection

Did I achieve my top 3 goals of the week? If not, why not?

....

....

....

....

....

What lessons did I learn this week that I can use to make next week better?

....

....

....

....

What am I proud of this week?

....

....

....

Notes:

....

....

....

7 WEEKS DOWN

You're getting there!

Planner Progress

70%

3 WEEKS TO GO

Keep up the spirit!

"Whenever you want to achieve something, keep your eyes open, concentrate and make sure you know exactly what it is you want. No one can hit their target with their eyes closed."
- Paulo Coelho

Weekly Preparation

My top 3 goals of this week are:

1. ....

2. ....

3. ....

Weekly Schedule

Monday	Tuesday	Wednesday

Thursday	Friday	Weekend

Habit Tracker

	Mo	Tu	We	Th	Fr	Sa	Su
	☐	☐	☐	☐	☐	☐	☐
	☐	☐	☐	☐	☐	☐	☐
	☐	☐	☐	☐	☐	☐	☐
	☐	☐	☐	☐	☐	☐	☐
	☐	☐	☐	☐	☐	☐	☐

Daily Preparation

Today's Date: ___ /___ /___

Goal Review:

....

....

....

My ABCDE List

A-Tasks:

1. ....

2. ....

3. ....

B-Tasks:

1. ....

2. ....

3. ....

C-Tasks:

1. ....

2. ....

3. ....

D-Tasks:

1. ....

2. ....

3. ....

E-Tasks:

1. ....

2. ....

3. ....

My Daily Schedule

Time
05:00
05:30
06:00
06:30
07:00
07:30
08:00
08:30
09:00
09:30
10:00
10:30
11:00
11:30
12:00
12:30
13:00

Notes:

....

....

....

....

....

....

Time
13:30
14:00
14:30
15:00
15:30
16:00
16:30
17:00
17:30
18:00
18:30
19:00
19:30
20:00
20:30
21:00
21:30

Daily Reflection

If I had to rate my day (1–10): _____

Did I achieve my top priorities today? If not, why not?

....

....

....

....

....

....

What lessons did I learn today that I can use to make tomorrow a better day?

....

....

....

....

....

....

What am I proud of today?

....

....

....

....

Daily Preparation

Today's Date: ___ /___ /___

Goal Review:

....

....

....

My ABCDE List

A-Tasks:

1. ....

2. ....

3. ....

B-Tasks:

1. ....

2. ....

3. ....

C-Tasks:

1. ....

2. ....

3. ....

D-Tasks:

1. ....

2. ....

3. ....

E-Tasks:

1. ....

2. ....

3. ....

My Daily Schedule

05:00
05:30
06:00
06:30
07:00
07:30
08:00
08:30
09:00
09:30
10:00
10:30
11:00
11:30
12:00
12:30
13:00

Notes:

....

....

....

....

....

....

13:30
14:00
14:30
15:00
15:30
16:00
16:30
17:00
17:30
18:00
18:30
19:00
19:30
20:00
20:30
21:00
21:30

Daily Reflection

If I had to rate my day (1–10): _____

Did I achieve my top priorities today? If not, why not?

....

....

....

....

....

....

What lessons did I learn today that I can use to make tomorrow a better day?

....

....

....

....

....

....

What am I proud of today?

....

....

....

....

Daily Preparation

Today's Date: ___ / ___ / ___

Goal Review:

....

....

....

My ABCDE List

A-Tasks:

1. ....

2. ....

3. ....

B-Tasks:

1. ....

2. ....

3. ....

C-Tasks:

1. ....

2. ....

3. ....

D-Tasks:

1. ....

2. ....

3. ....

E-Tasks:

1. ....

2. ....

3. ....

My Daily Schedule

05:00
05:30
06:00
06:30
07:00
07:30
08:00
08:30
09:00
09:30
10:00
10:30
11:00
11:30
12:00
12:30
13:00

Notes:

....

....

....

....

....

....

13:30
14:00
14:30
15:00
15:30
16:00
16:30
17:00
17:30
18:00
18:30
19:00
19:30
20:00
20:30
21:00
21:30

Daily Reflection

If I had to rate my day (1-10): _____

Did I achieve my top priorities today? If not, why not?

....

....

....

....

....

....

What lessons did I learn today that I can use to make tomorrow a better day?

....

....

....

....

....

....

What am I proud of today?

....

....

....

....

Daily Preparation

Today's Date: ___ /___ /___

Goal Review:

....

....

....

My ABCDE List

A-Tasks:

1. ....

2. ....

3. ....

B-Tasks:

1. ....

2. ....

3. ....

C-Tasks:

1. ....

2. ....

3. ....

D-Tasks:

1. ....

2. ....

3. ....

E-Tasks:

1. ....

2. ....

3. ....

My Daily Schedule

Time
05:00
05:30
06:00
06:30
07:00
07:30
08:00
08:30
09:00
09:30
10:00
10:30
11:00
11:30
12:00
12:30
13:00

Notes:

....

....

....

....

....

13:30
14:00
14:30
15:00
15:30
16:00
16:30
17:00
17:30
18:00
18:30
19:00
19:30
20:00
20:30
21:00
21:30

Daily Reflection

If I had to rate my day (1–10):

_____

Did I achieve my top priorities today? If not, why not?

....

....

....

....

....

What lessons did I learn today that I can use to make tomorrow a better day?

....

....

....

....

....

What am I proud of today?

....

....

....

....

Daily Preparation

Goal Review:

....

....

....

"Great things are done by a series of small things brought together."
- Vincent Van Gogh

My ABCDE List

A-Tasks:

1. ....

2. ....

3. ....

B-Tasks:

1. ....

2. ....

3. ....

C-Tasks:

1. ....

2. ....

3. ....

D-Tasks:

1. ....

2. ....

3. ....

E-Tasks:

1. ....

2. ....

3. ....

My Daily Schedule

| 05:00 |
| 05:30 |
| 06:00 |
| 06:30 |
| 07:00 |
| 07:30 |
| 08:00 |
| 08:30 |
| 09:00 |
| 09:30 |
| 10:00 |
| 10:30 |
| 11:00 |
| 11:30 |
| 12:00 |
| 12:30 |
| 13:00 |

Notes:

....

....

....

....

....

....

| 13:30 |
| 14:00 |
| 14:30 |
| 15:00 |
| 15:30 |
| 16:00 |
| 16:30 |
| 17:00 |
| 17:30 |
| 18:00 |
| 18:30 |
| 19:00 |
| 19:30 |
| 20:00 |
| 20:30 |
| 21:00 |
| 21:30 |

Daily Reflection

If I had to rate my day (1-10): _____

Did I achieve my top priorities today? If not, why not?

....

....

....

....

....

What lessons did I learn today that I can use to make tomorrow a better day?

....

....

....

....

....

What am I proud of today?

....

....

....

....

Daily Preparation

Today's Date: ___ /___ /___

Goal Review:

....

....

....

My ABCDE List

A-Tasks:

1. ....

2. ....

3. ....

B-Tasks:

1. ....

2. ....

3. ....

C-Tasks:

1. ....

2. ....

3. ....

D-Tasks:

1. ....

2. ....

3. ....

E-Tasks:

1. ....

2. ....

3. ....

My Daily Schedule

05:00	
05:30	
06:00	
06:30	
07:00	
07:30	
08:00	
08:30	
09:00	
09:30	
10:00	
10:30	
11:00	
11:30	
12:00	
12:30	
13:00	

Notes:

....

....

....

....

....

....

| 13:30 |
| 14:00 |
| 14:30 |
| 15:00 |
| 15:30 |
| 16:00 |
| 16:30 |
| 17:00 |
| 17:30 |
| 18:00 |
| 18:30 |
| 19:00 |
| 19:30 |
| 20:00 |
| 20:30 |
| 21:00 |
| 21:30 |

Daily Reflection

If I had to rate my day (1–10): _____

Did I achieve my top priorities today? If not, why not?

....

....

....

....

....

What lessons did I learn today that I can use to make tomorrow a better day?

....

....

....

....

....

....

What am I proud of today?

....

....

....

....

Daily Preparation

Goal Review:

....

....

....

"The superior man is modest in his speech, but exceeds in his actions."
– Confucius

My ABCDE List

A-Tasks:

1. ....

2. ....

3. ....

B-Tasks:

1. ....

2. ....

3. ....

C-Tasks:

1. ....

2. ....

3. ....

D-Tasks:

1. ....

2. ....

3. ....

E-Tasks:

1. ....

2. ....

3. ....

My Daily Schedule

05:00
05:30
06:00
06:30
07:00
07:30
08:00
08:30
09:00
09:30
10:00
10:30
11:00
11:30
12:00
12:30
13:00

Notes:

....
....
....
....
....

13:30
14:00
14:30
15:00
15:30
16:00
16:30
17:00
17:30
18:00
18:30
19:00
19:30
20:00
20:30
21:00
21:30

Daily Reflection

If I had to rate my day (1-10): _____

Did I achieve my top priorities today? If not, why not?

....
....
....
....
....

What lessons did I learn today that I can use to make tomorrow a better day?

....
....
....
....
....

What am I proud of today?

....
....
....
....

Weekly Reflection

Did I achieve my top 3 goals of the week? If not, why not?

....

....

....

....

....

What lessons did I learn this week that I can use to make next week better?

....

....

....

....

What am I proud of this week?

....

....

....

Notes:

....

....

....

8 WEEKS DOWN

Awesome job!

Planner Progress

80%

2 WEEKS TO GO

Stay sharp!

"Life is not designed to hand us success or satisfaction,
but rather to present us with challenges that make us grow."
- Terry Laughlin

Weekly Preparation

My top 3 goals of this week are:

1. ....

2. ....

3. ....

Weekly Schedule

Monday	Tuesday	Wednesday

Thursday	Friday	Weekend

Habit Tracker

	Mo	Tu	We	Th	Fr	Sa	Su
	☐	☐	☐	☐	☐	☐	☐
	☐	☐	☐	☐	☐	☐	☐
	☐	☐	☐	☐	☐	☐	☐
	☐	☐	☐	☐	☐	☐	☐
	☐	☐	☐	☐	☐	☐	☐

Daily Preparation

Today's Date: ___ /___ /___

Goal Review:

....

....

....

My ABCDE List

A-Tasks:

1. ....

2. ....

3. ....

B-Tasks:

1. ....

2. ....

3. ....

C-Tasks:

1. ....

2. ....

3. ....

D-Tasks:

1. ....

2. ....

3. ....

E-Tasks:

1. ....

2. ....

3. ....

My Daily Schedule

Time
05:00
05:30
06:00
06:30
07:00
07:30
08:00
08:30
09:00
09:30
10:00
10:30
11:00
11:30
12:00
12:30
13:00

Notes:

....

....

....

....

....

| 13:30 |
| 14:00 |
| 14:30 |
| 15:00 |
| 15:30 |
| 16:00 |
| 16:30 |
| 17:00 |
| 17:30 |
| 18:00 |
| 18:30 |
| 19:00 |
| 19:30 |
| 20:00 |
| 20:30 |
| 21:00 |
| 21:30 |

Daily Reflection

If I had to rate my day (1-10): _____

Did I achieve my top priorities today? If not, why not?

....

....

....

....

....

What lessons did I learn today that I can use to make tomorrow a better day?

....

....

....

....

....

....

What am I proud of today?

....

....

....

....

Daily Preparation

Today's Date: ___ / ___ / ___

Goal Review:

....

....

....

My ABCDE List

A-Tasks:

1. ....
2. ....
3. ....

B-Tasks:

1. ....
2. ....
3. ....

C-Tasks:

1. ....
2. ....
3. ....

D-Tasks:

1. ....
2. ....
3. ....

E-Tasks:

1. ....
2. ....
3. ....

My Daily Schedule

Time
05:00
05:30
06:00
06:30
07:00
07:30
08:00
08:30
09:00
09:30
10:00
10:30
11:00
11:30
12:00
12:30
13:00

Notes:

....

....

....

....

....

....

13:30
14:00
14:30
15:00
15:30
16:00
16:30
17:00
17:30
18:00
18:30
19:00
19:30
20:00
20:30
21:00
21:30

Daily Reflection

If I had to rate my day (1-10): _____

Did I achieve my top priorities today? If not, why not?

....

....

....

....

....

....

What lessons did I learn today that I can use to make tomorrow a better day?

....

....

....

....

....

....

What am I proud of today?

....

....

....

....

Daily Preparation

Goal Review:

....

....

....

My ABCDE List

A-Tasks:

1. ....

2. ....

3. ....

B-Tasks:

1. ....

2. ....

3. ....

C-Tasks:

1. ....

2. ....

3. ....

D-Tasks:

1. ....

2. ....

3. ....

E-Tasks:

1. ....

2. ....

3. ....

My Daily Schedule

Time
05:00
05:30
06:00
06:30
07:00
07:30
08:00
08:30
09:00
09:30
10:00
10:30
11:00
11:30
12:00
12:30
13:00

Notes:

....

....

....

....

....

....

13:30
14:00
14:30
15:00
15:30
16:00
16:30
17:00
17:30
18:00
18:30
19:00
19:30
20:00
20:30
21:00
21:30

Daily Reflection

If I had to rate my day (1-10): _____

Did I achieve my top priorities today? If not, why not?

....

....

....

....

....

....

What lessons did I learn today that I can use to make tomorrow a better day?

....

....

....

....

....

What am I proud of today?

....

....

....

....

Daily Preparation

Goal Review:

....

....

....

My ABCDE List

A-Tasks:

1. ....

2. ....

3. ....

B-Tasks:

1. ....

2. ....

3. ....

C-Tasks:

1. ....

2. ....

3. ....

D-Tasks:

1. ....

2. ....

3. ....

E-Tasks:

1. ....

2. ....

3. ....

My Daily Schedule

05:00
05:30
06:00
06:30
07:00
07:30
08:00
08:30
09:00
09:30
10:00
10:30
11:00
11:30
12:00
12:30
13:00

Notes:

....

....

....

....

....

| 13:30 |
| 14:00 |
| 14:30 |
| 15:00 |
| 15:30 |
| 16:00 |
| 16:30 |
| 17:00 |
| 17:30 |
| 18:00 |
| 18:30 |
| 19:00 |
| 19:30 |
| 20:00 |
| 20:30 |
| 21:00 |
| 21:30 |

Daily Reflection

If I had to rate my day (1-10): _____

Did I achieve my top priorities today? If not, why not?

....

....

....

....

....

....

What lessons did I learn today that I can use to make tomorrow a better day?

....

....

....

....

....

....

What am I proud of today?

....

....

....

....

Daily Preparation

Today's Date: ___ /___ /___

Goal Review:

....

....

....

My ABCDE List

A-Tasks:

1. ....

2. ....

3. ....

B-Tasks:

1. ....

2. ....

3. ....

C-Tasks:

1. ....

2. ....

3. ....

D-Tasks:

1. ....

2. ....

3. ....

E-Tasks:

1. ....

2. ....

3. ....

My Daily Schedule

05:00
05:30
06:00
06:30
07:00
07:30
08:00
08:30
09:00
09:30
10:00
10:30
11:00
11:30
12:00
12:30
13:00

Notes:

....

....

....

....

....

| 13:30 |
| 14:00 |
| 14:30 |
| 15:00 |
| 15:30 |
| 16:00 |
| 16:30 |
| 17:00 |
| 17:30 |
| 18:00 |
| 18:30 |
| 19:00 |
| 19:30 |
| 20:00 |
| 20:30 |
| 21:00 |
| 21:30 |

Daily Reflection

If I had to rate my day (1-10): _____

Did I achieve my top priorities today? If not, why not?

....

....

....

....

....

....

What lessons did I learn today that I can use to make tomorrow a better day?

....

....

....

....

....

....

What am I proud of today?

....

....

....

....

Daily Preparation

Goal Review:

....

....

....

"How wonderful it is that nobody need wait a single moment before beginning to improve the world."
— Anne Frank

My ABCDE List

A-Tasks:

1. ....

2. ....

3. ....

B-Tasks:

1. ....

2. ....

3. ....

C-Tasks:

1. ....

2. ....

3. ....

D-Tasks:

1. ....

2. ....

3. ....

E-Tasks:

1. ....

2. ....

3. ....

My Daily Schedule

Time
05:00
05:30
06:00
06:30
07:00
07:30
08:00
08:30
09:00
09:30
10:00
10:30
11:00
11:30
12:00
12:30
13:00

Notes:

....

....

....

....

....

....

13:30
14:00
14:30
15:00
15:30
16:00
16:30
17:00
17:30
18:00
18:30
19:00
19:30
20:00
20:30
21:00
21:30

Daily Reflection

If I had to rate my day (1-10): _____

Did I achieve my top priorities today? If not, why not?

....

....

....

....

....

What lessons did I learn today that I can use to make tomorrow a better day?

....

....

....

....

....

....

What am I proud of today?

....

....

....

....

Daily Preparation

Today's Date: ___ / ___ / ___

Goal Review:

....

....

....

My ABCDE List

A-Tasks:

1. ....

2. ....

3. ....

B-Tasks:

1. ....

2. ....

3. ....

C-Tasks:

1. ....

2. ....

3. ....

D-Tasks:

1. ....

2. ....

3. ....

E-Tasks:

1. ....

2. ....

3. ....

My Daily Schedule

Time
05:00
05:30
06:00
06:30
07:00
07:30
08:00
08:30
09:00
09:30
10:00
10:30
11:00
11:30
12:00
12:30
13:00

Notes:

....

....

....

....

....

13:30
14:00
14:30
15:00
15:30
16:00
16:30
17:00
17:30
18:00
18:30
19:00
19:30
20:00
20:30
21:00
21:30

Daily Reflection

If I had to rate my day (1–10): _____

Did I achieve my top priorities today? If not, why not?

....

....

....

....

What lessons did I learn today that I can use to make tomorrow a better day?

....

....

....

....

....

What am I proud of today?

....

....

....

....

Weekly Reflection

Did I achieve my top 3 goals of the week? If not, why not?

....

....

....

....

....

What lessons did I learn this week that I can use to make next week better?

....

....

....

....

What am I proud of this week?

....

....

....

Notes:

....

....

....

9 WEEKS DOWN

You're almost there!

Planner Progress

90%

1 WEEK TO GO

Go crush it!

"The only difference between ordinary and extraordinary
is that little extra."
– Jimmy Johnson

Weekly Preparation

My top 3 goals of this week are:

1. ....

2. ....

3. ....

Weekly Schedule

Monday	Tuesday	Wednesday

Thursday	Friday	Weekend

Habit Tracker

Habit Tracker	Mo	Tu	We	Th	Fr	Sa	Su
	☐	☐	☐	☐	☐	☐	☐
	☐	☐	☐	☐	☐	☐	☐
	☐	☐	☐	☐	☐	☐	☐
	☐	☐	☐	☐	☐	☐	☐
	☐	☐	☐	☐	☐	☐	☐

Daily Preparation

Today's Date: ___ / ___ / ___

Goal Review:

....

....

....

"All life is an experiment. The more experiments you make the better."
- Ralph Waldo Emerson

My ABCDE List

A-Tasks:

1. ....

2. ....

3. ....

B-Tasks:

1. ....

2. ....

3. ....

C-Tasks:

1. ....

2. ....

3. ....

D-Tasks:

1. ....

2. ....

3. ....

E-Tasks:

1. ....

2. ....

3. ....

My Daily Schedule

| 05:00 |
| 05:30 |
| 06:00 |
| 06:30 |
| 07:00 |
| 07:30 |
| 08:00 |
| 08:30 |
| 09:00 |
| 09:30 |
| 10:00 |
| 10:30 |
| 11:00 |
| 11:30 |
| 12:00 |
| 12:30 |
| 13:00 |

Notes:

....

....

....

....

....

| 13:30 |
| 14:00 |
| 14:30 |
| 15:00 |
| 15:30 |
| 16:00 |
| 16:30 |
| 17:00 |
| 17:30 |
| 18:00 |
| 18:30 |
| 19:00 |
| 19:30 |
| 20:00 |
| 20:30 |
| 21:00 |
| 21:30 |

Daily Reflection

If I had to rate my day (1-10): _____

Did I achieve my top priorities today? If not, why not?

....

....

....

....

....

....

What lessons did I learn today that I can use to make tomorrow a better day?

....

....

....

....

....

....

What am I proud of today?

....

....

....

....

Daily Preparation

Today's Date: ___ /___ /___

Goal Review:

....

....

....

My ABCDE List

A-Tasks:

1. ....
2. ....
3. ....

B-Tasks:

1. ....
2. ....
3. ....

C-Tasks:

1. ....
2. ....
3. ....

D-Tasks:

1. ....
2. ....
3. ....

E-Tasks:

1. ....
2. ....
3. ....

My Daily Schedule

05:00
05:30
06:00
06:30
07:00
07:30
08:00
08:30
09:00
09:30
10:00
10:30
11:00
11:30
12:00
12:30
13:00

Notes:

....

....

....

....

....

....

| 13:30 |
| 14:00 |
| 14:30 |
| 15:00 |
| 15:30 |
| 16:00 |
| 16:30 |
| 17:00 |
| 17:30 |
| 18:00 |
| 18:30 |
| 19:00 |
| 19:30 |
| 20:00 |
| 20:30 |
| 21:00 |
| 21:30 |

Daily Reflection

If I had to rate my day (1-10): _____

Did I achieve my top priorities today? If not, why not?

....

....

....

....

....

....

What lessons did I learn today that I can use to make tomorrow a better day?

....

....

....

....

....

....

What am I proud of today?

....

....

....

....

Daily Preparation

Today's Date: ___ /___ /___

Goal Review:

....

....

....

My ABCDE List

A-Tasks:

1. ....

2. ....

3. ....

B-Tasks:

1. ....

2. ....

3. ....

C-Tasks:

1. ....

2. ....

3. ....

D-Tasks:

1. ....

2. ....

3. ....

E-Tasks:

1. ....

2. ....

3. ....

My Daily Schedule

Time
05:00
05:30
06:00
06:30
07:00
07:30
08:00
08:30
09:00
09:30
10:00
10:30
11:00
11:30
12:00
12:30
13:00

Notes:
....
....
....
....
....

| 13:30 |
| 14:00 |
| 14:30 |
| 15:00 |
| 15:30 |
| 16:00 |
| 16:30 |
| 17:00 |
| 17:30 |
| 18:00 |
| 18:30 |
| 19:00 |
| 19:30 |
| 20:00 |
| 20:30 |
| 21:00 |
| 21:30 |

Daily Reflection

If I had to rate my day (1–10): _____

Did I achieve my top priorities today? If not, why not?

....
....
....
....
....
....

What lessons did I learn today that I can use to make tomorrow a better day?

....
....
....
....
....

What am I proud of today?

....
....
....
....

Daily Preparation

Today's Date: ___ / ___ / ___

Goal Review:

....

....

....

My ABCDE List

A-Tasks:

1. ....

2. ....

3. ....

B-Tasks:

1. ....

2. ....

3. ....

C-Tasks:

1. ....

2. ....

3. ....

D-Tasks:

1. ....

2. ....

3. ....

E-Tasks:

1. ....

2. ....

3. ....

My Daily Schedule

05:00	
05:30	
06:00	
06:30	
07:00	
07:30	
08:00	
08:30	
09:00	
09:30	
10:00	
10:30	
11:00	
11:30	
12:00	
12:30	
13:00	

Notes:

··

··

··

··

··

··

13:30	
14:00	
14:30	
15:00	
15:30	
16:00	
16:30	
17:00	
17:30	
18:00	
18:30	
19:00	
19:30	
20:00	
20:30	
21:00	
21:30	

Daily Reflection

If I had to rate my day (1-10): _____

Did I achieve my top priorities today? If not, why not?

··

··

··

··

··

··

What lessons did I learn today that I can use to make tomorrow a better day?

··

··

··

··

··

What am I proud of today?

··

··

··

··

Daily Preparation

Goal Review:

....

....

....

My ABCDE List

A-Tasks:

1. ....

2. ....

3. ....

B-Tasks:

1. ....

2. ....

3. ....

C-Tasks:

1. ....

2. ....

3. ....

D-Tasks:

1. ....

2. ....

3. ....

E-Tasks:

1. ....

2. ....

3. ....

My Daily Schedule

05:00	
05:30	
06:00	
06:30	
07:00	
07:30	
08:00	
08:30	
09:00	
09:30	
10:00	
10:30	
11:00	
11:30	
12:00	
12:30	
13:00	

Notes:

....

....

....

....

....

| 13:30 |
| 14:00 |
| 14:30 |
| 15:00 |
| 15:30 |
| 16:00 |
| 16:30 |
| 17:00 |
| 17:30 |
| 18:00 |
| 18:30 |
| 19:00 |
| 19:30 |
| 20:00 |
| 20:30 |
| 21:00 |
| 21:30 |

Daily Reflection

If I had to rate my day (1–10):
_____

Did I achieve my top priorities today? If not, why not?

....

....

....

....

....

....

What lessons did I learn today that I can use to make tomorrow a better day?

....

....

....

....

....

....

What am I proud of today?

....

....

....

....

Daily Preparation

Today's Date: ___ /___ /___

Goal Review:

....

....

....

My ABCDE List

A-Tasks:

1. ....

2. ....

3. ....

B-Tasks:

1. ....

2. ....

3. ....

C-Tasks:

1. ....

2. ....

3. ....

D-Tasks:

1. ....

2. ....

3. ....

E-Tasks:

1. ....

2. ....

3. ....

My Daily Schedule

Time
05:00
05:30
06:00
06:30
07:00
07:30
08:00
08:30
09:00
09:30
10:00
10:30
11:00
11:30
12:00
12:30
13:00

Notes:

....

....

....

....

....

....

13:30
14:00
14:30
15:00
15:30
16:00
16:30
17:00
17:30
18:00
18:30
19:00
19:30
20:00
20:30
21:00
21:30

Daily Reflection

If I had to rate my day (1–10): _____

Did I achieve my top priorities today? If not, why not?

....

....

....

....

....

....

What lessons did I learn today that I can use to make tomorrow a better day?

....

....

....

....

....

....

What am I proud of today?

....

....

....

....

Daily Preparation

Goal Review:

....

....

....

> *"We generate fears while we sit.*
> *we overcome them by action."*
> *- Dr. Henry Link*

My ABCDE List

A-Tasks:

1. ....

2. ....

3. ....

B-Tasks:

1. ....

2. ....

3. ....

C-Tasks:

1. ....

2. ....

3. ....

D-Tasks:

1. ....

2. ....

3. ....

E-Tasks:

1. ....

2. ....

3. ....

My Daily Schedule

Time
05:00
05:30
06:00
06:30
07:00
07:30
08:00
08:30
09:00
09:30
10:00
10:30
11:00
11:30
12:00
12:30
13:00

Notes:

....

....

....

....

....

13:30
14:00
14:30
15:00
15:30
16:00
16:30
17:00
17:30
18:00
18:30
19:00
19:30
20:00
20:30
21:00
21:30

Daily Reflection

If I had to rate my day (1–10): _____

Did I achieve my top priorities today? If not, why not?

....

....

....

....

....

What lessons did I learn today that I can use to make tomorrow a better day?

....

....

....

....

....

....

What am I proud of today?

....

....

....

....

Weekly Reflection

Did I achieve my top 3 goals of the week? If not, why not?

....

....

....

....

....

What lessons did I learn this week that I can use to make next week better?

....

....

....

....

....

What am I proud of this week?

....

....

....

....

Notes:

....

....

....

10 WEEKS DOWN

Congratulations, you've made it!

Planner Progress

100%

10 WEEKS OF PEAK PRODUCTIVITY

Be proud of yourself!

You Made It!

Congratulations! You've made it to the end of the Peak Productivity Planner. Very impressive. You can be proud of your accomplishment!

I truly hope that you had an amazing experience and that the planner helped you get more done, be more focused, and feel more motivated. All in all, I hope that these 10 weeks have helped you live a more productive and goal-oriented life.

If you enjoyed this planner, please let me know!

I'd love to hear about the things you've achieved and the wins you've gained over these past 10 weeks. Reading about your success fuels my own flame, so please feel free to send me an email at: jari@thepersonalgrowthlab.com. I truly appreciate it, so don't hesitate to shoot me a message. I don't bite :)

I hope to see you around at Personal Growth Lab. We've got many other exciting courses, tools, and resources to help you be more productive!

To Your Personal Growth,

Jari Roomer
Founder Personal Growth Lab

PS. Turn to the next page and check out the special offer I have for you as a thank you for purchasing this planner...

"You are never too old to set another goal
or to dream a new dream."
- C.S. Lewis

Special Offer ->

See next page!

The 30-Day Productivity Challenge

Do you want to completely transform your productivity in
30 Days?

For 30 days, you will...

Get more done by applying <u>smart productivity techniques</u> every day.

Work with <u>laser-focus</u> and stop getting distracted.

Stop procrastinating and <u>take massive action</u> towards your goals (I guarantee, your to-do list won't stand a chance).

Whether you're studying for an exam, writing a book, or working on an important project.

The 30-Day Productivity Challenge gives you the productivity boost you need to get real results and make exponential progress.

Visit **thepersonalgrowthlab.com/courses** and use the code "planner" to get **25%** off your registration as a thank you for purchasing this planner!

Free Guide:
27 Productivity Hacks

I've got a FREE resource available for you that will help you boost your productivity:

Free Guide:
27 Productivity Hacks
For Superhuman Performance

In this productivity guide you will learn...

- How To Get More Results Without Working Harder or More Hours
- The #1 Trap That Kills Your Productivity
- The Truth Behind Why You Should Work Less Instead of More
- Easily Gain More Free Time (Guilt-Free)
- Achieve Your Personal & Business Goals 372% Faster

To download this free guide, go to:
thepersonalgrowthlab.com/free-resources

Printed in Great Britain
by Amazon